Grieve

Stories and Poems about Grief and Loss

Volume 7

Grieve Volume 7
Hunter Writers Centre
PO Box 494 The Junction
Newcastle NSW 2300

Email: publishing@hunterwriterscentre.org
Website: www.grieveproject.org

Grieve: Stories and Poems about Grief and Loss

22 21 20 19 18   1 2 3 4 5
ISBN-978-0-6484099-7-7(paperback)

Cover design by HWC Publishing
Typesetting by HWC Publishing
2019 Published by Hunter Writers Centre Inc.

© Each short story/poem is copyright of the respective author
© This collection copyright of Hunter Writers Centre

All rights reserved.
No part of this publication may be reproduced, stored in a retrieval system, or transmitted in any form by any means electronic, mechanical, photocopying, recording or otherwise without the prior consent of the publishers.

You are fading.
Not lost.
Just leaving.
A map being redrawn.

~

from *The Cartographer*
Frances Lovell

Table of Contents

Helpers Kate Littlejohn	2
Mourning Time Kirstyn McDermott	4
Incense John Foulcher	5
New Year's Day Ned Stephenson	6
Beautiful Rose B. Hansun	7
The Dance Zana Kobayashi	8
Cicada Wings Rico Craig	9
Niko Margaret Walker	10
My bro Janette Ellis	12
Coda Karen McCrea	13
Daughters Sandra Macgregor	14
The Last Conversation Amanda McDonald	15
Not Dead Yet Max Dibley	16
As Well as Can Be Expected Annie Bucknall	18
Thirty-one steps before I bury my sister Dan Shushko	20
Letter to my Mum Dianne Montague	22
Barb Leanne Coleman	24
Earth oven Isobel Hodges	25
Nine, Hillcrest Street Jessica Andreatta	26
After Words Carmel Macdonald Grahame	27
12 Weeks, Again Cate Kennedy	28

On Being Offered a Last Day Madeleine Dale	29
Baby Shannon Hayes	30
The Coolest Thing Ever Gillian Swain	31
Negative Mass Magdalena Ball	32
Agnes and Pa Kylie Shelley	33
Afterwards Janeen Webb	34
The Sorry Basket Nola Firth	35
An Imagination of Blessings Nikki McWatters	36
Salvage Zenobia Frost	37
Beginning of the End Judi Lane	38
Things I Couldn't Throw into the Skip Kerrie Nelson	39
Of Love & Physics Anna Murchison	40
Breath Melanie Zolenas-Kennedy	41
Lather Max Ryan	42
Gone But Not Forgotten Christeen Kaluaat	43
Grief Leanne Pettigrew	44
The Cartographer Frances Lovell	45
Tears and the Sea Julie Sladden	46
Pearl Grey Sara Crane	47
The Ones From Coles Nalin Jeenmuang	48
First day after Pam Schindler	49
I didn't mean for you to die Geoffrey Ahern	50

Father Laura Jan Shore	51
Hand Hygiene Jeanette Lacey	52
Meditation upon the passing of a day Claire Wilson	53
Heelys Elizabeth Kuiper	54
Her Name is Sarahjane Rebecca Gubalane	56
Before, During, After Sueanne Gregg	57
Intensive Care Lea McInerney	58
A wake for Amy Kerry Harte	59
Something I lost to the night Cheryl Howard	60
The Whisper Jannette Gibbons	61
No One Told Me That Grief Would Last My Entire Life Claire J. Harris	62
Light Carmel Macdonald Grahame	63
Love Hurts Caroline Freedman	64
Half-Life Denise	65
Teacher Niko Campbell-Ellis	66
Interior Castle Ann-Marie Blanchard	67
Letting Go Trish Bolton	68
On Love Paige Duffy	70
In That Desperate Hour Katheen Kituai	71
My Sister Robyn Moriconi	72
The Persistence of the Image Damen O'Brien	73
Not Scared of Flying CJ Vallis	74

How Not to Kill People (Notes) Cassandra Scott	76
The Window Across the Way Kristen Roberts	77
Now the Other One Sharryn Ryan	78
Epithelial Rose Lucas	79
Tram 86 Kirsten Krauth	80
Time Crept By Sophia Moore	81
On the Nature of Black Holes Ruth Gilmour	82
Sa tiyán ng lupà Ivy Alvarez	83
The Room Sarah Pye	84
Vanished Laura Jan Shore	85
Sunflowers Ingrid Birgden	86
Life Lessons Rosalind Moran	87
I am a Little Eye Breaking Shari Kocher	88
Brain Cancer Ellen Shelley	89
Foreboding Kim Waters	90
You Don't Die When You Want To Val Gadd	91
The Hoarders Linda Harding	92
Galloway The Poet Mj	93
The Problem of You Aimee Sargent	94
I'm losing my patients Hilton Koppe	96
Blackie Annette Mullumby	97
Pomegranate Ella Jeffery	98

Abandoned Theatre Carolyn Abbs	99
The Spare Room Harrison Saich	100
Effie (1900–1951) Beth Spencer	101
What remains Frank Russo	102
The Telling Steve Coates	104
Today We Should Have Elanna Herbert	105
Don't Let it Bring You Down Shaun Maguire	106
Dreams Hessom Razavi	107
Too Much For Words Fiona Murphy	108
In Tumult Kathryn Fry	109
The Window Narelle Absolom	110
The Secret Life of Mum Cindy Bennett	111
Sadness is a Long Tunnel Rose Lucas	112
Ready to go Alex Grantham	113
When Are We Women Kathryn Lyster	114
Want Jemma van Loenen	115
The Breathing Earth Kimberley Zeneth	116
What Jane will Never Know Heather Thomas	117
Visiting Mum Zoë Disher	118
Earthing Jane Frank	120
Departure Natasha Parnian	121
At This End of Times Elanna Herbert	122

Dad — 124
Emma Young

The Souls of Millions of Light Years Away — 126
Tristan Carey

Uphill Triolets — 127
Stuart Barnes

Rearranging the paintings — 128
Jane Frank

Life After Death — 129
Heather MacKenzie

My Grandmother, searching for words — 130
Seetha Nambiar Dodd

A Haibun For My Dying Mother — 131
Rosemary Harper

The Letting Go — 132
Bea Jones

You Came Home With Purple Hair — 134
Andrew Sutherland

There Let the Waves Lave — 135
Ela Fornalska

Moving Images — 136
Angela Gardner

Public Grief and Silent Grief — 138
Jadie Kew

The Red Scarf — 139
Janey Runci

The Ship — 140
Elisa Hall

The Boy on the Wall — 141
Carolyn Abbs

The River — 142
Rachel Ranton

The Thieves at the Dam — 144
Tric O'Heare

Grief is love — 145
Samantha Geatches

Introduction

Another year of the Grieve project has again seen hundreds of Australians from all over the world submit stories and poems expressing their loss or the experience of loss by someone they know.

Many writers tell us that even if their work is not selected for publication they still gain much from the process of expressing their thoughts and feelings in writing. Loss and grief is such a powerful emotion that writing can often clarify, sort, express and lay plain the turbulence, chaos and sadness that loss delivers.

This year we are thrilled to receive three donations for the *In Memoriam* section of the Grieve project—donated prizes from members of the public who wish to remember someone who died. Not only do the *In Memoriam* prizes give you the opportunity to honour a special person but they reward writers for their craft. Thank you again to all the sponsors of the 25 prizes and special gratitude goes to the judges who dedicate themselves to reading and re-reading all the works.

    Karen Crofts
    Director
    Hunter Writers Centre

From the poetry judges:

Being the judge of any competition is an honour and a responsibility. But to be entrusted with the poems for the Grieve Writing Competition was tremendously sobering. As judges, we felt the need to pace ourselves, so as not to become overwhelmed or numbed. Behind each poem was a deeply personal, vital struggle to bear witness to loss. We aimed to give each poem the respect and attention it so clearly deserved.

Grief has a way of scrambling our thoughts and our language. So it was profoundly moving to read these poems, which have grappled with the complexity of this fundamental human emotion in order to find some kind of order and beauty in language. Each and every poem did that in some way. But the poems which resonated most deeply with the judges were ones that took us unflinchingly into their experience and perspective, in moving and memorable turns of phrase. Reading them, we encountered grief with new eyes, ears, hearts and minds.

    Andy Jackson & Rachael Mead
    Grieve Poetry Judges, 2019

Awards

The National Association of Loss and Grief (NALAG) Award
Helpers by Kate Littlejohn

The Pettigrew Family Funerals Award
Mourning Time by Kirstyn McDermott

The National Association of Loss and Grief (NALAG) 2nd Award
Incense by John Foulcher

Good Grief Award—for a work about grief or loss other than death
New Year's Day by Ned Stephenson

All About Grief Award—for a work about grief or loss after the death of a child
Beautiful by Rose B. Hansun

Lifeline Hunter Central Coast Award
The Dance by Zana Kobayashi

Newcastle Memorial Park Award
Cicada Wings by Rico Craig

The Calvary Mater Hospital Pastoral Care Award
Niko by Margaret Walker

Hunter New England Health, Mental Health Services Award
My Bro by Janette Ellis

White Lady Funerals Award
Coda by Karen McCrea

Simplicity Funerals Award
Daughters by Sandra Macgregor

Mindframe Award
The Last Conversation by Amanda McDonald

Palliative Care NSW Award
Not Dead Yet by Max Dibley

The Blue Knot Foundation Award
As Well As Can Be Expected by Annie Bucknall

Lake Macquarie Memorial Park Award
Thirty-One Steps Before I Bury my Sister by Dan Shushko

National Centre for Childhood Grief Award
Letter to my Mum by Dianne Montague

David Lloyd Funerals Award (Newcastle and Hunter Valley)
Barb by Leanne Coleman

In Memory of Michael Burdett
Earth Oven by Isobel Hodges
prize donated by Vicki Laveau-Harvie

The Norman Beard Memorial Award
Nine, Hillcrest Street by Jessica Andreatta
prize donated by granddaughter Jessie

Auspsych Australia Award
After Words by Carmel Macdonald Grahame

Hope Bereavement Care Award
12 Weeks, Again by Cate Kennedy

In Memory of Nathan Charles Richter
On Being Offered a Last Day by Madeleine Dale
prize donated by Annette, Joe and Sarah Richter

Hunter Writers Centre Award
Baby by Shannon Hayes

Maclean's Booksellers Award
Equal winners:
Negative Mass by Magdalena Ball
The Coolest Thing Ever by Gillian Swain

Helpers

Kate Littlejohn

Two hour drive, two hour wait at the regional airport, one hour flight. My five month old baby hasn't cried once and I am ready to spend a blissful week with my bestie after months apart. I can't believe how lucky I am.

In the car, just out of the airport, my phone buzzes. Dad, urgent and panicky, two words that never accompany his voice.

'You need to get on a plane to Melbourne. It's not good. It's Mum.'

My entire body goes cold; I am frozen by indecision and stubborn denial. This can't be it.

Those words mark a line in my life. Before. And after.

Back at the airport. Virgin helpdesk. Tried to explain my situation without letting the rising panic show. The airline staff mirrored the panic on my face back to me.

They got me on a flight. Again, my phone buzzed. Dad's voice, straining under the weight of the words he didn't want to say.

'She's gone. I . . . I'm so sorry. Don't come to Melbourne. Just . . . find your way home.'

I broke.

A deluge of tears threatened as I looked up at these kind women who just wanted to help me. Somehow, they understood that I needed to get back to my original airport. I don't know how because I am certain I used no real words. They performed airport magic and got me on the next flight.

They showered me with airport food vouchers, not knowing what else to do for this young stranger falling to pieces in front of them. I couldn't remember what hunger felt like.

I sat alone on the crowded plane with Eva (who had been the perfect baby . . . babies always know). I held her, tears streaming silently down my face.

I wondered what the other passengers thought.

There was a woman sitting next to me. She was Mum's age.

As we approached our destination, Eva started to squirm. The woman asked gently if she could help. I gladly passed her over, feeling overwhelmed thinking about the logistics of what was to come and overcome by just how wrong this day had gone.

She cuddled her, sang to her, soothed her. All the things my Mum loved to do. All the things she would never do again.

This stranger gave me space. She gave me time to pull myself together; time to breathe. I don't think I even thanked her.

It will remain the single most devastating day of my life. But without the helpers, it would have been so much worse.

People helped me that day in ways that they probably won't ever know. Their kindness carried me through the darkness. Total strangers.

I remember them every day; it replays in my mind like clockwork. I wonder if they remember me. If they know what they did for me that day. I wonder what their names were.

My mum's name was Maree. She was a helper too.

Mourning Time
Kirstyn McDermott

My friend's cat, Gin-Gin, rolls over and I rub her belly with my bare foot. Her fur is warm, sun-drenched, soft as those plush toys you find at airports. I've agreed to take Gin-Gin after Inez is gone. It might be months, or weeks. Her oncologist doesn't know, so neither do we.

Inez scribbles a note on the page she's reading and turns it over. She left the university at the end of last semester but still edits for friends, and has a paper of her own she wants to finish. This isn't that. It's a draft from a former student who doesn't even know Inez is ill.

Ill. Such a slim, slippery eel of a word. Inez is dying. My friend is *dying*, and if some green-gilled postgrad thinks he has a right to even a millisecond of the time she has left—

'Why didn't you say no?'

'I would have,' Inez says, 'if I didn't want to do it.'

'You don't have to waste your time on shit like this anymore.'

Inez puts down the paper and stares out across the native bushland metres from the veranda where we've spent the morning. It's not a huge patch, with a new development soon to shrink it further, but it's the reason she bought the house a decade ago. Close by, blue wrens chitter in the scrub. Later, a pair of kookaburras will alight on the railing to demand their evening treat of raw beef.

'People imagine, if they get cancer or something, they'll quit their jobs, sell up and spend their last months living large, travelling the world, eating all the cake, whatever.' Inez shrugs, looks back at me. 'But you don't. At first, because of hope.

The hope that you'll beat it, that you can beat it, and then because . . . this is your life, and it means something. So you grieve, every day, but you go on. Doing the things that matter. Seeing the people you care about. Because there's no other choice. You know this.'

At work last month, a colleague threw down the latest issue of *Biological Conservation*. 'The insects are dying,' he said. 'We're all fucked.'

The insects are dying. It's the most terrifying sentence any of us should ever want to hear. I made my fair-trade coffee and returned to my desk. Continued to comb through the latest data on this year's fire season—the worst on record, until the next time. Ate my line-caught tuna salad, trying not to picture the mass fish kills along the Murray.

The insects are dying.

You don't have to waste your time on shit like this anymore.

But we do. We do. Even as we grieve this passing world, we must live in it.

Here on the veranda, Inez tilts back her head, closes her eyes; I follow suit. The sun warms our faces. Stretched at our feet, Gin-Gin purrs.

Choiceless. Grieving. Determined. We go on.

Incense
John Foulcher

I recall how we queued to see Notre Dame,
how we shuffled below the rose windows
in that hollow between prayer and stone
and the clerestory saints. Sitting for vespers,
the singular, unsullied tones of a language
neither of us knew, though the sense of it settled
among the souvenirs, the relics and cameras,
the cobalt blue of the virgin at the portal window.

Trudging the stairs to the lair of gargoyles
to see Paris from the angle of angels, its bones;
standing among bells. The vast bass bell,
Emmanuel, could ring out only for moments,
its stone-shuddering Gothic gong a threat
to holy height. I think something came to you here,
a kind of belief, that buttressed you, years later,
as cancer caressed you with its bony hands. . .

This morning, news of burning, footage
of the steeple in flames, snapping like a twig,
pouring its transient gold into the empty nave.
The plundering smoke, the glassed-in gospels gone.
Where we'd sat among the chanting, only rubble.
The past will always be past. Once loved,
things become incense, lingering in the space
where we held them and knew them and let them go.

New Year's Day
Ned Stephenson

The farmer rested his high-powered rifle on the seat beside him and closed the truck door. His jaw was set and his brow creased as he started the engine. Soil weathered hands held the steering wheel as he passed the woolshed yards, his eyes distant and sorrowful, it would be a long drive out to the backcountry, and he hoped three boxes of bullets would be too many.

He drove across sparse paddocks long eaten to the ground and cobbled dry creeks. Any closed gate he came to was left open afterwards. As the country steepened, he shifted into four-wheel drive, at least now the hill track was easy to navigate without long grass hiding the stones. He wished they were hidden again.

The resinous eucalypt scent of the hills had been replaced by the smell of smoke. It had been a hot fire; a grass fire would only brown the leaves of the trees, this had been a real forest fire and only the heaviest branches and ash remained. When he saw the first animal, he stopped and got out. From a distance, he could see the scorched flesh of the half-burnt sheep. The animal did not move as he approached and raised his rifle; there was no delay, only a slap against his shoulder then a crack that echoed across the hills. The farmer made no sound as he walked on, the swish of ash under his boots replacing the usual snap and crunch of the undergrowth. Further on more animals were huddled against a fence, trapped with no escape as their flock had cooked alive. None remaining moved as he shot them one at a time, around the fence the air smelled of flesh as well as smoke.

Haunted the entire drive back to the homestead, the farmer did not remove his boots at the door and his wife was looking at the entrance to the kitchen when he came in. She asked him, and he replied by taking a hand from his pocket and dropping rifle shells on the kitchen table. His wife watched as they clattered and rolled against the crockery. So many, she said. Then he put his left hand into his other pocket and pulled out more shells, carefully adding them to the pile. Both of the woman's hands went to her mouth.

Not speaking, the farmer went through to his office beside the kitchen, put the rifle on his great-grandfather's desk and quietly shut the door. In the kitchen, the farmer's wife saw the ash on the tiles and began to sob.

Beautiful
Rose B. Hansun

In our small, two-storey home is a couch so worn, the leather curls away in parts like an orange peel. It sits upstairs where we cook and brew tea and fold up on its tired cushions content with silence—our cradle for hollow lovers; a witness to our weathered souls. Night matures and the promise of rest beckons us off its lap to a simple oak bed. We lie, tangled, in wait of sleep to hasten the sunrise.

By dawn's exuberant light a new day presents, replete with second chances. We try again, my blue-eyed soul mate and I, determined to draw out more meaningful moments—fleeting permissions to forget and be happy, found in ordinary things: an impromptu outing, a solemn act of kindness. When they can only be found in quiet days at home, our cat with the pelt of a lynx drapes approvingly over our thighs. A paragon of solace, stretching regally, the king of our affections.

He arrived shortly after life caved in; just when we needed a small, eccentric companion to dote on. Months earlier, we would never have considered adopting an animal. We were eagerly anticipating another addition to our family. Her name came easily. She was nothing short of exquisite. Beau, French for Beautiful, the captor of our hearts; a miracle knitted in the warmth of my flesh, until one day, she moved with a soft rush of sparks.

At just over five months, pursued and snapped by a swooping ultrasound probe, black and white images of her magnificent form were handed to us. She pouted in one, hid behind her raised fist in another. We coursed with love and awe and overwhelming desperation to keep her safe. Alive. At six months she was born with a labouring heart and saw nothing of our devastation before quietly slipping away. The fourth to be lost and now, no more.

Beau. Beautiful. The reason for our race to togetherness. On an average day, when work swallows up our choicest hours, evenings become a spectacle of impulsive hugs, kisses on foreheads and silken fur, and simple dinners made with devotion. Weekends wash away the frenzied week through surfs and foaming coffees and pursuits of whim. And only in those sacred moments, when it feels safe to exhale, do we acknowledge the rougher days, when despair erupts into trembling sobs and emptiness entombs us in our own bleak worlds. Where we pause mid-conflict to acknowledge the weight of living incomplete and search for ever elusive words of consolation.

We see our cracks, wide and raw, and turn ourselves inside out to fill them. We beg each other's forgiveness. Often. We look to her death to better understand life. And though our motley crew is not as we dreamed, we are still a family, a fragrant arrangement I cherish above all else—my blue-eyed soul mate, our lynx-of-a-cat and a heaven-bound wanderer called Beautiful.

The Dance
Zana Kobayashi

Without fail, when my world falls quiet, my mind will wander to meet you—to dance with your memory. For the first few years, I couldn't stand to face you so I'd fill my schedule to the brim with noise and commitment, my pain wanting to drown you out. I would push myself into new worlds and forms, there were times I wondered if you would recognise me. There were many times I barely recognised myself.

I still remember the physicality of losing you. My brain slowed right down, as if a world without you wasn't worth being processed. Colours faded, the noise muted, I couldn't seem to follow conversations to their end. Sentences melted into my grief. My back would ache as though my insides had died along with you, my spine no longer strong enough to hold me upright.

I bought a pregnancy test the day after you died, the morning your sister called to tell me. During that strange day before I knew, I'd felt faint and almost vomited in the gardens of an art gallery. As I pulled the box out of the slippery plastic I hoped I had somehow managed to keep a part of you with me. But instead, as the faint sky-blue line appeared, I realised it was my body telling me you had left.

We had counted my menstrual cycles as a way of keeping track of time. We celebrated each bleeding as reprieve from parenthood. After that day I found myself counting to keep track of a child that hadn't even existed.

I feel differently now, of course. I no longer want to scream into the earth like we did the New Years after your death. Unable to bring ourselves to celebrate that terrible year, as midnight was counted in, we gathered away from the party in a dark paddock and began to scream. First into the skies, then into the earth, my fists beat into the soft ground. I'd never heard such guttural sounds escape my mouth before. But it felt more right, and perhaps did me more good, than the previous ten months of tears and therapy.

Three years later, as I lie in a bed inside a house you will never visit, my heart is still with you. And I find myself wondering what the next step is. How long is it appropriate to love a dead man? How long do I stay in love with you, longing for your skin and your secret whispers?

I imagine loving you as a crinkled old woman while you remain young and immature. It makes me feel sick. But not as sick as the thought of not loving you at all. Because it's not about wanting to wish it away, I would never wish you away, not even the parts that hurt me.

So I have committed myself to this quiet dance with you. A few steps forwards with one step back to meet you, always.

Cicada Wings

Rico Craig

They say the youngest child dies
on a Sunday. I wish I'd beaten more time
into your chest. Our twenties were carved from dust;

a decade living casual, lugging bubble-wrapped computers,
drinking gin from Solo cans while we waited
in loading bays for delivery trucks to arrive.

The best nights were spent in parked cars, telling lies
to shoestring glamours with tatts on their wrists;
they held your baby-face like a favourite knife.

You collected friends, hoarded each breath
in your shoebox full of cicada wings.
You told me how insects got caught in stone,

preserved between layers of rock. You'd open
the box, get me to hold my hand close,
palm above, and tell me how their fascination with air

kept you alive nights. No one will say what happened
to you. It's hard. Your mother is a broken cigarette,
gummy eyes, a menagerie in her chest.

She poured the best part of her memory into your heart,
it wasn't enough to keep you straight.
For two days she's been sitting with Aunty June,

down your street, they're wailing
into crying towels, rags around their necks
drenched in tears. They've cried scar trails

into their chests. When boys die, she wants them
to be reborn, slippery, as men,
incisor missing, blood on their chin.

They've stopped saying your name, all
they do is croon baby sounds.
Me and the girls are down by the creek

with flashlights, stamping thunder from the ground,
trying to find a place for your wings.

Niko
Margaret Walker

Red, constant.
 Escape, none.
 Death, ever present.
The blazing sun of my country's flag, perfect and eternal, envelopes my existence. That was my life once, perfect and eternal, but no more. The gloom of war turned everything to darkness, and red, always red. Children, my classmates, on work detail, built fire breaks from rubble. Relentless but important work. Just a precaution we thought, the war was truly upon us, we will do our duty. We are surely close to victory. My beautiful friend Niko helped make the hard work bearable. She had a way of lighting up my life. Her name means 'red child'. I can still see her laughing as we worked under the luminous blue sky, sharing our lunch. We would hold hands as we scampered to the ferry to our work deployment, to our doom. Niko had a gentleness which I loved to watch from afar as she performed her duties at the Shinto shrine as a Miko—a shrine maiden. Clothed in red and white, she lived out her secret life of spirits, spells and dancing for the dead. How could we know we had so little time left? The bombs fell elsewhere, so we thought. How could we know 34023'N 132027'E was a lucrative target for Uncle Sam.

The faint blue sky dissolved into night at 8:15am. 'Little Boy' crushed little children, extinguished my friends. My Niko, gone. Instantly. No more blue sky. The whistle, the rumble, the blast—red. The billowing toxic clouds—red. Scourging acid rain—red. Relentless radiation burns—red. Screaming in the street, screaming in my home, screaming in my head. Screaming with our throats red.

Why was I spared? My appendix scar, at the time, an inconvenience that kept me from my friends, Niko and duty to my country. Now, a severe red line. A constant reminder of what saved me that day, now haunts me forever. The scar that divides my world into before, after and forever.

Before, when I was hopeful for my world. Before, when Niko was alive and laughing. Before, when the sky was blue.

After. After the bomb. After stars and stripes ripped my world apart. After the clouds shrouded my perfect world.

Forever. Forever missing Niko. Forever knowing I survived while others perished. Forever seeing the perfect red circle of my flag, mocking me, looking like a bomb, a sick joke for all the world to see.

They call this survival, but it feels like death. An ever-present shame of being alive. As I trace Niko's name on the stone memorial in honour of my classmates, a tear runs down my cheek into the ruby earth. I must live on for Niko. I must be her Miko as she was for others at the Shinto shrine. I must speak on behalf of the spirits of the dead. Clothed in red and white, I will tend the graves of those whose lives were obliterated from this world.

    Red, continues.
    Escape, slowly.
    Death, not yet.

My bro
Janette Ellis

I dyed my hair black when I was fifteen. It looked awful against my Casper white skin. Desperate to improve the situation before I saw my then-crush at the school disco, I used colour stripper to conjure back my mocha locks. I was left with a brittle, orange mess. In tears, I burst into my older brother's room and begged him to drive me to the chemist for hair dye. He jumped up and grabbed his keys. That's the kind of brother he was. Seven years my senior, gentle, wise, funny, a seriously talented artist and always there for me. He called me sis. I called him bro.

But he was a conundrum. Sometimes the lovable brother, other times someone else. He'd cross the line then keep moving. His big brain constantly worked against him. For weeks at a time he'd stay in his room, angry and silent. He couldn't settle. A brilliant HSC result was followed by two false starts at university. A gallery owner offering him his first solo show precipitated another long, dark period. Nothing was good enough. He destroyed much of his own work.

I moved interstate. In his thirties, he left home and set up house with a cousin. He got a job and coasted into something like independent life. It didn't last. By the time I returned, he was back home, convinced he had a terminal disease. No specialist could find anything wrong, but he quit his job and his life contracted. He told me he was taking something that helped. I didn't ask what. I should have. It was Ativan, the most addictive benzodiazepine. Supposedly a short-term fix, he was on it for over a decade. Then it stopped working.

He spiralled. My family and I didn't know how to help. It ended with him perched on a cliff in the Blue Mountains, sending us a suicide note by text. He didn't jump but that's when we lost him. Our new reality is a haze of psychiatric clinics, ECT, medications and furiously treading water, trying not to be sucked under ourselves. Physically tackling him when he was in the grip of psychosis to stop him harming my parents was my lowest point. It felt like forever till the police came. My brother wouldn't do these things.

I don't recognise him now. He looks similar, but heavier, sadder, slower. Like a clone that didn't turn out right. A pretender. Call it his soul or his essence, something vital is gone. I look into his eyes but can't find him. There are still times something compels him back to the clifftop. His psychiatrist says people often work themselves up to it, the act of leaving. Mental illness and drugs stole my brother, leaving behind this shell. Mourning someone who is still there is like lying on the grass watching clouds drift past. Where was the beginning? Where is the end? I don't know. I just know that I miss my bro.

Coda
Karen McCrea

Packing up your house, we frowned over the old Arabica,
decided yes, we really should keep the small crystal ware
and the teacups that were your grandmothers,
the doorplate from your Greek house,
the chairs from your Italian villa, the table from Spain,
these, the tokens of your best adventures belong with us, yes.

The stuff of your life was put to trial as we sorted,
'keep', 'throw'—and guilty, we tried to hide our acts of disposal,
so as not to pain you as you sat amidst the chaos,
forebearing, keeping good form, as you always did,
while your life was undone around you,
pretending the reckoning was not upon you,
though your sharp *'don't throw that away'* betrayed
your blind eyes seeing more than you allowed us to know,
saving us from saving you.

The dust of all desires may be long settled,
but still, these things tell a long, rich, life well lived,
and how must it have been for you to let go of it all,
a great and ruthless release of every binding and beloved thing.
How was it for you as we looked for the perfect emblematic thing
to keep you with us when you became made of memory alone?
You knew we did it, and we knew these things,
the coda of your living, could not be the thing itself. You.

You gathered your rare courage then, left your house,
reconciling one kind of home for another,
and in this relentless passage, still found, somehow, the light.
It was in you, annealed, yes,
burnished into all the grace that made you.
And then the only thing left was love,
grown far deeper than the numbers of its years,
carrying you through the long, long hours of these last days,
back to unbeing,
where now you rest in endless loving memory,
and shadows and shimmering reminiscence
must be enough, for you are beyond us all.

Daughters
Sandra Macgregor

Your hand in mine is cool, the nails pale and short. I cut them for you only yesterday, in the ward; cut them, filed them, applied lotion lovingly to your fragile, suffering skin. Chemo has left its mark everywhere.

My own hand wears its neglect: the nails chewed, chips of blue in the centre of each. *I will never wear this colour again.* We bought this nail polish together, giggling at how a mother and daughter could be so close as to have matching nails. Best friends. Forever.

Your arm is thin; each bruise knocks against my heart, testimony to the battle nearly over. *How did we get here so quickly?* I brush your hair back from your forehead, the grey strands silky between my fingers. *Open your eyes Mum, just one last time.* But you will never look at me again, I know. I am here just waiting, until there is no more I can do for you. This is my last labour of love. Five months of fighting for you, and now I will hold your hand till it is over. You will not be alone and I need to be with you. I cannot imagine this world without you.

I stroke your hair, marvelling at its beauty, even at this stage. Suddenly, I am thinking of Patricia. I wonder, for the umpteenth time, if her hair is thick like yours, silky like yours. Today, this thought is unbearable. You lie here motionless, forced asleep till the inevitable last breath, and my heart clenches. Patricia. You've only glimpsed her once in your life, that day in the hospital nursery. They denied you at first. *Clean break,* they said. You insisted; she was held up to the window and you'd looked, then walked away. *What else could you do?*

You were sixteen. No parents, no support, no protection. *Unfit*, they called you. It took years to throw off the shame and track her down. But she did not want to be found. Her words slashed as deeply as the wound made by losing her in the first place.

'She's frightened, Mum.' How else to explain the rage unleashed on those pages?

'I just wanted to tell her the truth. We don't know what she's been told.'

My fingers ached to turn the letter to dust. 'I think we can guess.'

Yet now, I feel sorry for her. She's missed an opportunity to meet the most wonderful person and put to rest the demons that are obviously eating her alive.

I gently kiss your forehead, check that you are comfortable. *No pain,* they said, when they brought you here. *We aim for no pain.* If only that could have been the story of your life. I lay my head on your chest, listen to the steady beat of the heart that will soon be silent. Tears slide over my nose, onto your nightie. I will not leave you. No more pain. My wish for you, my darling mother.

The Last Conversation
Amanda McDonald

The nightmares are always the same. I'm pleading with her, reaching out to her, grabbing at her hands, and physically trying to hold her back from what she is about to do. All the things that I wish I had done, and would have done, had I known that my best friend was about to take her life that night.

I talked to her on the evening of her death. She was upset about something, and I tried to comfort her down the phone line, from kilometres away. I was in a new-mother fog, with a five week old baby. My daughter was crying. 'I'll call you later tonight'. I said. 'Or tomorrow', thinking about how long it might take to get the baby off to bed. We said goodbye and my friend's voice cracked a little. Then the baby cried some more and the phone call was over.

I didn't call my friend back that night. Nor would I ever speak to her again. Her mother told me the next day that she had died by suicide that night, after calling her friends to say goodbye. Had I known the purpose of her call I would have been on the next flight out to see her, would have pleaded with her, reached out to her, grabbed her and held onto her—all the things I do in my nightmares now. Too late.

It's over two years now since that last conversation. I have a beautiful two-year old daughter who will never know her mum's best friend. The uneasy peace I have made with the night of my friend's death is periodically shattered—by nightmares, by a sudden thought of her, the memory of her voice, a conversation with her mum, or a glance into the endless depths of sadness in her father's eyes.

Every media report of suicide brings a new rush of helplessness. As though somehow my friend's death should have been the last. Because how could such a needless loss happen again? And again? I think of the many others who have walked and will walk this path of loss. I feel my breath catch in my throat, and I have to sit down. I breathe in the suffering of the bereaved, and I breathe out compassion and love. And I remember the friend who slipped from my grasp.

Not Dead Yet
Max Dibley

'Not dead yet?'

She returned his half-hearted smile.

'Not yet.'

He wanted to run to her. Instead he shuffled through the doorway, past poles and flashing machines. Bent to kiss her. Winced.

Damn beds. Too low. She seemed weaker.

'Brought you something.' Gently lifting her head, he slid the pillow into place. She nestled back into the feather-down.

'Thanks Dad. Smells like home.' He pulled up a chair, gesturing at the garish balloons.

'Visitors?'

'Yeah. Some of my kids.'

Get Well Soon: a flamboyant smear of crayon and sparkles.

'I . . . haven't told them yet.'

He nodded. *My kids.* No children of her own, yet a mother to so many. It would break their hearts.

Once he'd hoped for a grandchild. But life had other fortunes in store and she'd been only too happy to be swept along in its embrace: study, travels, friendships, heartbreaks. Then the teaching job and 'no time for serious boyfriends', and now here she lay with a mass the size of a soccer-ball where a baby should grow.

Inoperable, they'd said. The surgeon. His adoring entourage.

How silently furious he'd been with them all.

'Guess I'll meet her soon,' she murmured. 'Mum.'

His mind wandered off: another time, another hospital bed.

'It'll be wonderful,' he managed. 'She'll give you one of her big hugs. Bombard you with questions!'

They held hands in silence: thick, punctuated by the beep of sombre machines.

I'm scared Molly. When you arrived your mum left, and I thought I'd die too. But you rescued me. Such joy born of such despair. And now, you too . . .

He smiled faintly.

'Brought you something else.'

He hesitated. Showing her might reveal more than he could bear.

She took the photograph from his trembling hands. He saw her eyes go wide with the same delight as the child in the image. His tears came then and he stared at the floor.

'I remember!' she sighed. The girl on the man's knee, sunlight streaming onto wild curls, mouth agape as she turned to watch him. She couldn't have been more than five, and he'd been, what . . . forty? Barely even grey. One hand around her tiny waist, the other cradling the object of her fascination: a fiddle, the fine rich grain visible even now.

'I'd sit on your knee and you'd play for hours . . .'

Every Saturday. Sundays too, if Martha had visited in his dreams. He'd play and he'd sing and he'd teach her all the old tunes. Time would stop, the sadness would pass, until it was just sunlight and music and his beautiful girl, her laughter the promise of life to come.

'What was that song?' she murmured. 'The one you always sang.'

She leaned back into her pillow, breathed in the flavour of happier days. A tiny feather escaped from the seam. Entranced, weary and terrified, he watched it lazily circle her face. It danced and spun, so beautiful and fragile.

And from deep down inside came the stirrings of the old song . . .

As Well as Can Be Expected
Annie Bucknall

When I was twelve, the sudden passing of my grandmother turned my grandfather's salt-and-pepper hair pure white. He awoke the morning after her death to a pillow littered with the last of his proud grey strands and a pain in his back so severe, his shoulders set themselves into a permanent stoop. Grief had spirited away the pigment from his life and turned his remaining years into dull shades of black and white.

But it doesn't always.

Sometimes, it sharpens your vision until you're viewing your life on some monstrosity of a television, unable to turn the contrast down.

Unable to switch it off.

My wife, Merryn, emerges from our ensuite in full technicolor, her chin held high. The look she gives me dares me to comment, goads me into starting another argument with her I don't have the strength to finish. These past three weeks, a vacuum-sealed bag has closed around our marriage and I have to take small, shallow breaths to keep myself from suffocating.

She's wearing a crumpled outfit straight from our daughter's dirty clothes basket; her once-blonde hair is now the purple hue of a fresh bruise . . . she even smells like Kayla's perfume. I want to beg her to take the clothes off, to put on one of the dozen corporate suits that hang pressed in her closet. But the firm set of her mouth freezes my words before they form.

This isn't just an outfit. It's combat fatigues.

'When he looks at me from the dock today, I want him to see Kayla staring back. I want him to remember.' Merryn's hand strays to the tomato sauce stain on our daughter's jeans—a blood-coloured remnant of her stolen vitality. 'I want him to suffer.'

She smooths out my suit jacket and pins a purple ribbon on my lapel.

'Me too,' I say.

And it's true. But I envy her fury. Where she has anger, I have only my grandfather's shameful resignation and a new, dreadful understanding. It wasn't my grandmother's death that turned my grandfather's hair white . . . it was the painful realisation that when it counted most, he couldn't protect her. That the love that had carried them through their lives together was powerless to save her.

At the peal of the doorbell I turn away, leaving Merryn to gather her things.

My pale-faced parents are huddled under our front awning, trying to escape the drenching rain. I usher them in, grateful that the wet weather has kept the reporters off our front lawn today.

Mum holds me as she cries and I take comfort in the open expression of her sorrow, allowing her to feel this moment for the both of us. Gathering herself together, she wipes her tears from my cheek. 'How are you both holding up?'

Merryn appears in the hallway—a ghoulish spectre of our teenage daughter—and their eyes widen.

'As well as can be expected,' I say.

Thirty-one steps before I bury my sister

Dan Shushko

Step 1: Brush my teeth before I put on my shirt.

Step 2: Find a tie that's not too black.

Step 3: Open the pair of socks she bought me for my last birthday.

Step 4: Sit on the bed for a minute.

Step 5: Try to remember whether I had a coffee this morning.

Step 6: Put the shirt on.

Step 7: Turn off the Spotify playlist that's been playing for days.

Step 8: Think of all the people that will come to the funeral that don't need to be there.

Step 9: Lean against the cupboard door, look at my phone and scroll through some messages.

Step 10: Decide not to wear cufflinks.

Step 11: Think of my nephew who is now sitting in an emptier home. He lost his mum, I only lost my sister.

Step 12: Put some music back on because I don't want to listen to the birds in the trees.

Step 13: Hate my brother-in-law for dancing with the stripper at his buck's show. Wonder if my sister ever found out?

Step 14: Know that I went to a Catholic School for 13 years and the only thing that I can remember is that the 'Lord giveth and the Lord taketh'.

Step 15: Choose a different tie.

Step 16: Feel sadness for my brother-in-law. Know that he is a good man who just lost the closest friend he had.

Step 17: Hear the phone ring. Let it ring through.

Step 18: Sit back down on the bed.

Step 19: Hear the phone ring again. See that it's my mother. Answer it. It's the same question that she had last night.

Step 20: Know that my mother will soon bury her only daughter.

Step 21: Regret yelling at the florist for getting the wrong colour balloons.

Step 22: Remember how much my sister teased me when I brought home the girlfriend who wore a beret. What did she call her? A French twat?

Step 23: Think about a trip that I might go on when this all dies down. Maybe find some peace somewhere near Kosciuszko.

Step 24: Forget for a second how to do up a tie.

Step 25: Feel guilty for thinking about a mountain and not my sister.

Step 26: Wonder whether I've checked my work emails enough whilst I've been away.

Step 27: Cry a little.

Step 28: Put an extra hanky in my pocket.

Step 29: Sit quietly on my bed because I don't want to go.

Step 30: Straighten my tie.

Step 31: Get up and leave.

Letter to my Mum
Dianne Montague

Dear Mum

It's a long time since I've spoken to you. Your face is dim and blurred. Is the image a memory, or just a remembered photograph that sits between the smelly pages of one of those albums? You would have looked at that album when I was a child, seen your photo and grimaced. You might've even asked me to tear it up. What a miracle it was that I didn't.

I'm twenty-six years older than you now. It's strange being older than your Mother. When I hold your photo up next to my face and stare into the mirror I see no likeness. Why didn't you give me those bright blue eyes and that curly brown hair? At least then I would feel like your daughter.

Our time together was so brief; it's hard to remember it. You were this bubbly, swirl of perfume, dashing off to some outing—always wearing matching shoes, bag, hat, gloves and perfect lipstick. Every morning I'd watch with amazement as you filled the space defined by your lips with the dazzling red. To finish it off you would open your mouth just a little to wipe your lips with your poised pinkie.

When I was thirteen you married my stepfather. You also became very ill. He was there to look after you and I faded into the background. Everything else seemed to come first. The operations, the radiotherapy, the new marriage, all contrived against me. Books gave me solace. I escaped into books that took me away from my life with cancer and a sick mum.

The three years you were sick I blossomed into adolescence, while you lost your bloom altogether. The greyness of cancer filled your being and our lives. I finished school and went to work. I discovered that life was a bit hard. I wanted your hugs but you were so brittle I thought you would break.

The phone call came while I was working in that job I disliked. No one knew at work. Back then we didn't talk about cancer. I don't think people knew what to say. I certainly didn't know how to tell them. The days of sharing feelings and support groups were way off in the future.

I raced to the Hospital just up the street. You were in a large ward with dozens of other women. The curtains were around you. I wanted to hold you and tell you all sorts of things. I wanted you to hold me and tell me all sorts of things. We didn't hug and I didn't say goodbye. How could I fit sixteen years into one moment?

I missed that hug. I'll miss it forever.

I can give it though, that motherly embrace, that smothering, warm, 'you're important' embrace. My children are hugged often. We chat about all sorts of things, important or not. They're nearly as old as you and I'm still here.

Barb

Leanne Coleman

I followed Barb into the house. It was sparsely furnished. Dust covered the furniture and the lounge and chairs were tired, dirty dishes were piled in the sink. Barb told me to sit at the kitchen table and made us both a coffee before sitting down herself.

'You knew Christopher, did ya?' said Barb.

'Not really well, just saw him around and had the odd 'hello', that's all. He always seemed a nice kid.'

Barb gazed into her coffee.

'He was a great kid.' A tear rolled down her cheek as she continued. 'I was so proud of him, he was such a clever kid. When he was younger, Christopher would always come home from school and chatter like a monkey telling me everything he could think of about his day.'

'Then he went to High School.'

Barb got up and went to a shelf above the heater. She took down a photo and brought it to show me.

'That's the last photo I have of Christopher—school photo.'

The photo showed a thin, blond teenager with a shy smile.

'He changed a lot. He would just sit in the chair, quiet. I tried to get him talking but he'd only answer with one word answers.'

Although tears now rolled down Barb's cheeks she had a determined set to her mouth. I didn't know what to say; I don't think she would have heard me anyway. The story of Christopher—a grim rosary she needed to recite. Each word relived the devastation of her within. All I could offer her was my presence.

'One day I followed him home from school in the car. I saw them—kids—a few of them. They followed him, called him names. If they had touched him, I would have run them over. But they didn't.

'I wish to God I had now. Jail's better than this. At least those bastards wouldn't bother Christopher or God-knows-who-else anymore. Christopher would still be here.

'I went to the school to see what I could do. Useless. Just told me he was a shy kid and other kids would pick on him because they did that to everyone.' Her abrupt silence transcended words. Moments later, she took a deep breath, her words a blow to my senses.

'I found him. My beautiful boy.'

Our coffee grew cold in front of us both.

Her stillness shouted at me, demanding acknowledgement of the bleeding wound Christopher's death had inflicted on her.

The shadows in the room were lengthening, the afternoon was drawing to a close. None of us moved, I had to go. I was teaching in the morning.

I stood up.

'I have to go now.'

She didn't speak or move and I shut the door quietly behind me.

Earth oven
Isobel Hodges

Preparation begins by heating
the stones.
Next, lay the food down
cover with earth
and leave for many hours.

I slide the tube behind your ear
the device cycles
a mechanical meter.
If it can't detect breath
it will dispense air
unabated
until your lungs catch up.

Your lungs won't catch up.

I rub your spotted arms
and kiss your forehead.
I scratch your stubble
and you smile, say,
I'll shave tomorrow.

I long to crawl into the pit
with the yams and the fish.

I don't know how this will end/
I know how this ends.

Nine, Hillcrest Street
Jessica Andreatta

Friday mornings, Mrs M goes to the library to take up where she finished the week before. *Knitting* in nonfiction; *SWE* in fiction; foreign languages or large print—wherever it is she was up to. Electronic media and books for the young: the only exceptions to her rule. As someone checking each and every spine for something they are yet to read—or someone in search of a title piquing—she runs her finger along each book of every shelf until she comes across that for which she is searching: a book out of place.

She takes it out, turns it over, reads the blurb and inside cover.

'One.'

She replaces the book in its correct position and continues from the space left behind. Number by number—or letter by letter, depending—finding and replacing until she comes to a ninth, misplaced. The ninth book of the day is the one she borrows.

Her house is number nine. Nine, Hillcrest Street.

Mr M bought it for them both when they were married saying as they signed the papers, 'Nine seems a nice round number. Round as its bottom front step.' And there is the ninth of the ninth, Mrs M had replied when it came to her turn with the pen. Mr M nodding and knowing: theirs—an early spring wedding.

Fifty-nine years and nine months.

How cruel it seemed, Mr M said, that he should be going ahead of her. 'On the ninth of all things,' at a whisper. But Mrs M only smiled, the sort she reserved for him alone, when it was he would make her morning tea with lemon.

She stroked his cheek and caught his leaving. 'In the hands of Grace,' she said—holding his in hers. And though he was gone she sat alongside, catching his warmth as it ebbed and doing her best to take it all in.

She holds his warmth in her shadows, like a rounded front step in an afternoon turning to twilight. As such, it simply is. The ninth. The ninth she holds to breast, walking home with it resting against her, beneath a grey knitted hat; beneath a waning sun.

After Words
Carmel Macdonald Grahame

I sit on a bench reading to the sound of the break.
Words roar across the pages despite his too few birthdays.
Here he is, blowing out candles one at a time, counting kisses,
and by dwindling light making secret, knife-edged wishes.
The poems are young, and already they speak of love and grief.

The beach is a study in light and dark—
gull on one leg, on a pole, asleep; stone pylon like a pen in ink;
concrete walls-up the swell, slabs of weed meet an arc of waves.
This morning people came, bearing witness to time breached,
as his father and mother buried him.

She sat, my open-hearted friend, who wanted me to read these,
watching young women she did and didn't know line up,
their so-many fistfuls of dirt and petals tossed, overcome,
first loss amplified in hymns they didn't know existed,
learning that no one is immortal after all, and if not him, not them.

Young men without reason to know how the real thing is done
composed themselves in postures of grief, deliberate and grim,
like the syringes his broken sister found beside him.
His nervous brothers manned up, lowering unfamiliar weight down
between the headstones of an old crowd, planting him.

Words failed his father, who handed out roses and rosemary
and stared into scent-filled baskets, as if reasons might be found there,
for how a family comes to be deciduous.
Now, a man walks to the shore, waves to no one in particular,
a swimmer laps from nowhere to nowhere and back.

On the horizon a palisade of sticks is not, in fact,
But is an island refracting and not quite disappearing
in the heat and light that fracture distance.
Nothing seems to be what it is, is what it seems to be.
Even the gull has not moved, although it could fly.

Same-as-ever, this place, as flat and hot and dry
as if he'd never been here, or still is.
It really makes no difference now it seems to me,
whether the poems sink or swim.
They matter anyway; they overflow, they think.

12 Weeks, Again
Cate Kennedy

It's a small hospital, but no matter, they're doing their best, and it's not easy to find a bed quickly for an admission of a panicked woman already resigning herself to losing another one, walking stiffly with the big pad stuffed between her legs in a useless attempt to stem bleeding, there is nothing for it but to climb onto the bed which crackles with the blue plastic waterproofing because you are not the first to miscarry, not by a long shot, and someone's got to strip these sheets, sometime; some other woman, on a weekend shift, who you don't know and never will, because by the time she comes on you will be back home, emptied, shaking, blacking out dates in your diary, ashen, ashen.

It's not like they can give you a pill to stop it or reverse the process or even give any kind of reassurance because these things are out of our hands, they are in nobody's hands, they slip through the hands of the universe like slippery fluid and tissue, a knot that did not hold, and what can the nurses do except just leave you alone because they see the tears trickling down into your ears and into your oily Saturday morning hair as you lie there just waiting to be the vessel of it, bracing, it is something passing through you the way a storm passes through a spindly tree, a lesson in bracing, in abject bowed powerlessness.

But still, a small hospital with limited facilities, so it is nobody's fault in the partitioned room next to you a man is being administered to by the doctor and you can hear every word, although they are speaking in low voices, they are undemonstrative men, this doctor and this plumber, and the doctor is explaining the anaesthetic eyedrops he is about to administer to the man who just this morning was mucking about with his toddler who'd jumped onto his own bed at home and in the ruckus had scratched his dad's cornea. Just this morning, before somebody picked up pyjamas off the floor for the wash and made a list for the supermarket and warm small bodies breathing toast and milk and weetbix had tossed themselves reckless onto their parents, a sprawling hug towards Dad and a scratched eye and I would give anything.

Anything.

To be in that other bed with a scratched cornea and a child who longed to hug me waiting at home. What is it I can give? Tell me. It is yours.

These are the parameters of loss, to look squarely into your scoured future and catch a glimpse of your true shape waiting for you there as the nice guy and father of two in the bed on the other side of the partition says thanks mate, that's so much better, and the doctor says wait here and I'll write you a prescription, and you can get to the chemist before it closes.

On Being Offered a Last Day
Madeleine Dale

If I ever went back,
or you did,
I would want it to be
interstitial
without the burden
of expected departure
without the burn
of disinfectant still
in my nostrils;
the ashen hands, the
knowing.
I want that time
when we belonged only
to each other,
when there were no
bald spots on the fabric
of the sky.
There would be
nothing to cherish,
no bittersweet twist
to your mouth,
my hands. Only
this sense of eternity
unfolding before us
unbroken and
ignorant, once more.

Baby

Shannon Hayes

The months slip by, unchanging. Pages of the calendar fall as steady as autumn leaves, a promise of the cold, hard fingers of winter, waiting to prey on the bones of little birds—fallen, frozen, from the sky. The lump of your belly grows smaller, the stretch marks remain. All that time spent preparing for sleepless nights, all that waiting, to be left empty-handed.

It is the silence that hurts the most. You wake to crying in the night—needed—to realise it was a dream. A dream-turned-nightmare, each time stolen from you again. You float through the house like a wandering ghost, a lost ship in the fog. No beacon of light comes to your rescue.

You find yourself here once more, always here, anchored to the chaos of expectation. Who knew four small walls could house such cruelty, in shades of pink and blue. This room is a warzone of unused things. You kneel amongst the clutter of provisions: a changing bassinet heaped with nappies bought on sale; a pile of unwrapped gifts; an empty crib nestled with pristine soft toys—a golden bear with outstretched arms and a snow-white bunny with floppy ears. Both should be chewed and dribbled on by now.

'We'll try again,' he tells you, holds you like air. You are a skeleton in his arms. When did you last eat, last sleep? The night walking and daydreaming all blurs into one, a long road through the darkness, always searching for something to hold. The clock-hand in the kitchen is stuck ticking on the spot, its rhythm holds the missing beat. He didn't have a name. You wanted to meet him first, to see his face to know for sure. If only you knew then how hard it would be, to name a stillborn child.

The picture frames hang empty, once full of purpose and potential, now useless. They wait in vain for silly smiles, grubby fingers, milk-moustaches, all those precious moments robbed from you. When did you feel that last kick? Blank sheets of beige and white stare back at you from behind the glass. How you wish you could feel as empty as those frames. Grief is not emptiness. Grief is drowning in sorrow, with no words able to penetrate the surface through the ever-rushing stream,

The Coolest Thing Ever
Gillian Swain

Your mum laying out the tooth
brushes   we'd chorus and frothy giggle
the barbies and the soldiers on night duty
we   pyjama-clad   slept all in
tucked up and storied

on sleeping bag nights the bottom half stayed empty
legs too short to fill
I used-to think the model aeroplanes hanging from the ceiling
were the coolest thing ever

like the way your bed moves up and down like
all the colours the flowers bring to
this grey room
and us three all in hospital blankets
tucked up in beds and couches
talking at four a.m.   when nurses break the quiet of sleep
to do their checks
the indicators of dying need measuring
the measures of grief need
interrupting   the dawn is storied now
and stirs with our giggles this

sleepover is breathtaking   who'd ever have thought we'd
get to do this again   all craggy and almost fifty we
three here together for all
the wrong reasons
this can't be all there is

Negative Mass
Magdalena Ball

The brief pause between breaths
is the opening, involuted
it has an oily scent: deadnettle, Patchouli
ambushing me around a corner
while I was otherwise distracted

the morning is full of it, in the forest
sound breaks through fog
opens out into canopy
the way the world continues
with just the shadow of that smell
lingering like a note

vibrating at a frequency
only the dead can hear

echoing from the past
as light travels through the galaxy
over vast distances so what you see
looking through the mind's Hubble
is life, physical and conscious
still nurturing

the report comes in megaparsecs via
the Virgo Cluster, 60 million light-years
from the Milky Way, five years after I last
saw your body, not yet cremated
no longer in pain

pulsing with maternal energy
a Tabla rhythm against my grief
drumming with all the complexity
of your missing heat.

Agnes and Pa

Kylie Shelley

Agnes' pa used to embarrass her. Even in ICU he embarrassed her—the scent of unwashed hair and old cigarettes, the tatts from his navy days and the answers she had to give the organ donation nurses. They couldn't use his organs in the end but she kept his handprints and locks of hair in a sealed envelope, a tangible memory in shades of black, white and grey.

She had thought people in their fifties recovered from heart attacks. The news slowly trickled down to her, though—when he didn't wake up; when the ECG showed that his heart had recovered but the EEG showed that his brain had not—that he would not. She was bouncing her one-year old boy on her knee. His head was resting on her rounded belly. She reminded the doctor that just hours after he'd been admitted—once his tubes were in and she'd been able to see him—when he'd heard her voice, her pa had tried to sit up. He had looked into her eyes with intention and tried to say her name. The doctor shook his head and looked out the aluminium framed window at an autumn blue sky.

The day before they turned his life support off, Agnes begged the nurse for more time. She shook her head. 'Our first priority was saving his life, now our first priority is protecting his dignity. He wouldn't want to live like this, would he?' Both sets of eyes rested on Agnes' pa. Agnes shook her head. He wouldn't have, he'd said so himself. She took the nurse's words—not tangible like the sealed envelope, but a sentiment from the time nevertheless—and hung on to them.

On the tenth day the sound of the Muslim call to prayer resonated throughout the city. It was part of an arts festival. Agnes got ready and drove to the hospital to the hum of the call. Once there she held her pa's hands for the last time as the priest delivered his final rites. Watching his face fold, she thought of Sundays the most. Sometimes they had gone to church. Mostly they had drunk tea, played records and piled crumpled linen into the wicker washing basket. Once it had been washed they had hung it out and let it dry in its own time. She had loved breathing it in when it was all windswept.

Hospital white curtains offered them a private enclosure to face death in. The curtains breathed deeply as the nurse, head bowed, closed them. Agnes held her pa as he took his final breaths. They were shallow, shaken and laboured. Almost as soon as his life support was turned off, they stopped. Agnes' cries were high pitched and orphaned, contorted by filaments of disbelief. They—father and daughter—became continents separating; landmasses that had been interlocked for as long as she had lived, shifting involuntarily as the Earth rotated around them.

Afterwards
Janeen Webb

Last night, I visited my parents in Hades.

I drove in twilight through familiar suburban streets, across the river to my childhood home. I let myself in through the back door, as I always had done. There was a dog waiting for me, wagging his tail—not the black-and-white fox terrier of my childhood but a different, soft brown dog. I fed him anyway. He let me pass.

My parents were in the kitchen, as they always had been. Dad was in summer shorts, braces and a singlet: he was sitting at the kitchen table, reading the newspaper; Mum was wearing a patterned house dress, and was looking for something in the pantry. The room was dimly lit, as if by candlelight, though there was no candle. All the colour had been leached out, leaving a shadowy, sepia kitchen. My parents were clear and solid enough, but they seemed subdued, almost vague.

My father stood up and hugged me tight.

'We miss you,' he said.

'I miss you too,' I replied. 'Every day.' I breathed him in—his sweat-smell was right, comforting.

Mum smiled.

I crossed the kitchen and hugged her too, inhaling her favourite scent—the sweet scent of apple blossom.

Everything seemed normal—except we all knew they were both dead. It didn't matter. Mum put the kettle on, as she always did.

Somehow, we forgot to make the tea. We just sat quietly at the table, being together. Mum held my hand.

After a while, Dad spoke again. 'You have to go,' he said.

'I know.'

I hugged him again and Mum too. Then I went out through the back veranda. The dog was still there, still wagging, so I refilled his bowl and gave him a last pat before I left.

Outside, it was completely dark. The driveway was blocked. I couldn't get out.

I thought I saw a light flicker behind me so I went back inside to make sure my parents were still all right.

It was a mistake.

The dog was gone. My parents were gone—they'd been replaced by another couple, a couple wearing the same clothing, posed in the same positions in that same sepia kitchen. But now the room smelled different, smelled wrong.

'Who are you? What do you want?' the man asked.

'I'm sorry,' I said. 'I was looking for my parents.'

The woman understood. She nodded. 'We're waiting for our son,' she said.

My moment had passed. I turned away and crossed the dark yard again, ducking under the sagging rotary clothes line to reach my car. This time, the driveway was clear.

The night had turned cold.

As I drove away through the dull, aching emptiness of limbo, a dank mist was rising. I could only see a little distance: my headlights blurred. I looked in the rear-view mirror: the house was gone. Behind me, the road was disappearing into darkness.

The Sorry Basket
Nola Firth

She left me a sorry basket,

finely woven, patterned, with room for

the possibility of completion,

for escape from the fire in the playground—my own hair also alight,

for the question: where could she possibly go?

Space for the soaring blue iridescence

of the death

in three billion years

of the sun.

There was also a pebble,

a coral bone and an everlasting daisy.

An Imagination of Blessings
Nikki McWatters

I am electrocuted by grief. My hair is as stiff as burnt grass and my blood is dried up and flaking like tired paint. This grief coagulates in my marrow. It snakes through my nerves like acid and makes me tremble with pain. Tears burn my eyes.

I haven't even met you and don't know your names but I grieve for you in a reverse déjà vu sort of way. You, the grandchildren I will never know. I feel you in my dwindling DNA.

At night I don't sleep for thoughts of you as I stare out of my hospital window. I reach for you into the future but your faces flap away like invisible ghosts past an unfinished skull of moon. My blankets are heavy, my bed made of stone. I will miss soft white bread rolls and splashing in the surf. I will miss your grandfather, your mother and strong coffee. I will miss getting grey hair and wrinkles. But most of all I will miss you.

I imagine the tinkle of your laughter. First steps. Grandparents Day at school. Your finger-paintings and your graduations. Weddings. Great-grandchildren. Hugs.

The pain of not knowing you beats me with blunt fists and bruises me deep purple. It hurts. It's raw and cruel.

Will you look like me? Will you wonder about me? Will you see photos and imagine being wrapped in my arms? Will you ask why I look so young for a grandmother? Will they tell you because the grandmother part never happened for me? Old age, considered by fools to be a curse, is a gift I will never receive. I bite down on my mortification and taste salt. Blood or tears? I think of you most in these dark, lonely hours with the tinny sound of steel trays and trolleys rattling up and down the antiseptic hallways.

I will never buy you teddy bears. Never spoil you behind mummy's back. Never give you ice-cream for breakfast. Never slip a few sneaky dollars into your pockets after a visit.

My sore fingers crochet frantic bunny rugs that I'll never get to wrap you in. But I weave my hopes and dreams for you into the wool. I hope they will keep you warm. I'll sing you invisible lullabies.

Grandchildren of the future, know that I hold you in the palm of my heart. To you I will be just a photograph. Just a smiling two dimensional stranger. Someone that your family will try to recreate with dusty memories but will never quite capture. Grandma. Gone-too-soon-Grandma.

But I will love you from the stars. For eternity. All of you. My heart, my blood. My grandchildren.

   I will dream of you into the great wide forever. Sometimes perhaps, you might think of me. All we have is an imagination of blessings. I long for you from your past. But you are my future. All that will be left of me one day, is you.

Salvage
Zenobia Frost

That eye sees it all unfold again from the bang—
stars singeing. The membrane of my father's eye
flexes in the socket of a gelding skull, blood
rushing thick with big-screen oxygen. I'm ready
for my close-up. Mum always said

I look more like him when sleeping. I have to imagine
the doctors unhinging the mechanics of his look: never
smiling in photos, staring right through me, always weeping
in old spaghetti westerns when good wins out at last.

There is so much he had said he'd show me
out there. His eyes were already closed
when we arrived; it was his open mouth
we had to contend with, that burgundy void,
the vain gust of oxygen turned up to 11.

Beginning of the End
Judi Lane

Your t-shirt hangs over the kitchen chair. It makes me laugh until I cry.

Red flag. Blue and white cross. Grey printed slogan. A Nick original. Your take on the obligatory souvenir t-shirt. A generous t-shirt for a sizable man—wit and intellect to match. When worn, it stretches across broad shoulders. Clings to the hint of a belly that enjoys good food and great beer. On me, it is a black dress reaching my knees in loose folds. A hint of heady muskiness. Enough to bury my nose in and inhale you. The memory of your birthday. The final stop on the 'Nick is turning 60' road trip.

Eerie blue light where the sky never darkens. Snow and ice, slick sludge. Crisp cold tingling the nose, crystallizing the breath. Heat escaping in puffs through doors of stiflingly hot bars and shops. Golden lights twinkling from windows. Welcome to Tromso, Norway—home of the Northern lights.

Giddy with excitement, laughing as we try to keep our balance on black ice. Tickets for dog-sled rides purchased. A tour to chase the northern lights. Two things on the birthday bucket list we've travelled so far for. We do neither.

You sit at the wooden table. Street lights cast an amber glow through the apartment window. In the cramped kitchen space, I prepare dinner. Pieces of fish, pickled ginger, some nori. A Norwegian nod to sushi. The plates clatter as I place them between us.

And then, it starts. A strange look on your face, mouth moving, body tense, right arm twitching. I am aware of each nuance. Instinctively know to be able to describe all is important. Your body relaxes. Captivating blue eyes willing me to believe everything's alright. So *you* to pick up on *my* distress. A random collision of words—incomprehensible coming from your brilliantly articulate mouth and mind. Rich baritone voice trying to convey a soothing message. What comes out is 'make beautiful orange.' Mind and mouth at odds with each other. Later, we will name this 'Nicklish.'

In one cataclysmic evening, my role of wife is stripped from me. Your losses will be far greater.

'Tumour. Approximately nine centimetres. Low-grade astrocytoma, probably transformed.' Delivered in a soft, Norwegian accent. A foreign doctor speaking foreign words. They swirl with icy tentacles. Impact like an ice-pick to the soul. Snow-melt mind trying to grasp what he means. What *this* means. Wanting to wrap you in invisible threads of love, protection, and warmth. A shield against what is being thrown at us. Already feeling you slip away. Watching for signs that you are hearing something different to me. Hoping I have it wrong. I don't. The seizures followed by the 'Nicklish' speech are just the beginning.

The only northern lights we get to see are the fluorescents of the Tromso hospital.

Your t-shirt makes me laugh until I cry. It reads, 'I went to Tromso, Norway and all I got was brain cancer.'

Things I Couldn't Throw into the Skip
Kerrie Nelson

Their wedding telegrams
His scout's badge and jamboree songbook
Her Girls Own Almanac, 1938

Their broken bedroom barometer
      (red and green arrows missing)
His framed business registration
Her workplace training program:
      (Transactional Analysis for Managers)

Their mortgage discharge papers
His first pilots' licence
Her golf clubs

Their Morris Oxford Owners Manual
His plastic sandals
      (for fishing, Burrendong Dam)
Her easels, paints and brushes

His father's cutthroat razor, the strop
Her book of Scottish psalms
The receipt for their burial plots

Of Love & Physics
Anna Murchison

the night of the day you died, the moon came up huge and full—a blaze of orange in a cloth-hung sky—and I thought, as I have often done, that no one lived is ever gone. you were there in the moon as you are here upon my tired skin, and in the dirt and the dinner and the driving rain and in the hither-slick of engine oil I narrowly avoided as I drove our warring children home. such things are these confirm (much as your betrayals did) what I know of love and physics—which is,

they are one and the same.

Breath
Melanie Zolenas-Kennedy

My baby is four and a half months old. It is mid-May. It is eleven degrees. The main part of the church is weakly bolstered by air conditioning. We are not in the main part of the church. We are in a tiny stone alcove just to the side. I'm confused about its purpose. It is not a confessional. It is not the sacristy. It is just a tiny rectangular space, unilluminated and rough with cold.

My baby is four and a half months old and my body is rebelling against me. It exists only for her. My chest is swollen with what feels like thousands of pinpricks. I can feel the letting down seep into the sticky undersides of the maternity pads in my bra. The baby is on to me and she heaves herself towards me, mouth already open. She snatches at my woolly black jumper.

This is not a nursing-friendly jumper. In fact, I despise this jumper, with its long feathery fluff and high rounded neck. I had not known I would need a church outfit so soon.

We are in this little room because the baby was starting to fuss and claw during the ceremony. At first, I stumbled out of the pew with her and stood awkwardly bouncing to the side. But her cries grew more persistent, more insulted, so we went off in search of a different kind of sanctuary. One that would accommodate both a hungry baby and a poorly chosen jumper.

In this dark space, I realise that I am completely unprepared. I balance my baby in the crook of my left arm while I tug my jumper up. The brace of the air hits my still-raw stomach. The ancient and sickly smell of incense drifts in and around us. I think I may vomit. I think I may faint.

The baby will not vomit. The baby is such a pro. She latches on fiercely. I've forgotten my nursing shawl. There is no place to sit. I make sure that no long woolly jumper fibres get into my baby's mouth.

For three nights I haven't slept more than fifteen minutes in a row. The baby has. She's fine. I am not. I finally dragged her cot next to my bed so that I could sleep with my arm wedged in through the bars of the cot. So I can feel the rise and fall of her breath always.

For days, a vague terror has been in my heart. I have clung to the possibility that this has all been a huge misunderstanding and that everything would eventually be put right.

But now, in the church, I understand that nothing will be right—truly right—ever again.

The baby is now full. She and I step out of our little sanctuary. I clutch her. I've forgotten my jacket and gloves. My skin stings in the harsh chill. My breath puffs out white and grey, evaporating like ghosts.

Lather
Max Ryan

Each day after breakfast the old man comes
to the hospital with the morning paper

and a Gladstone bag full of shaving gear. His
son is dying, the nurse tells you. A tumour

on the brain. Weeks later, across the aisle
on your own bed you will glimpse, in the arc

of a flashlight, his newly bandaged head
and ashen skin before the pad of feet and ring

of winding curtains. But every morning the old
man brings the newspaper his son will be the first

to open and seats him on a chair in the concrete
courtyard and listens while his son reads out some

piece of news and the father quietly shuffles
around him and in one unbroken motion wraps

a white towel over his chest and neck and dips
a shaving brush into a mug of hot water. You can

tell the old man has done this many times in other
places but now this time is the only time. Now there

is only winter sunlight bathing a courtyard wall
and the background hum of General Ward 10

as an old man rubs a cake of soap into smooth
white froth to dab onto his son's fresh stubble

and, with one hand lightly cupping his jaw, scrapes
at the skin of the upturned face of the man become

a boy again with the just-whetted edge of a thin
curled blade before the lather can harden and dry

Gone But Not Forgotten
Christeen Kaluaat

Just before midnight ushered two police officers into my home where they calmly told me my darling son had chosen to end his life at 7.50 that night, on a lonely stretch of road just five kilometres from our home. It was Saturday the seventeenth May 1997. Just as calmly they explained Andrew had suffered severe soft tissue loss and I could not view him until 10.00 am the following morning, at the morgue. And then they left. They called to destroy me and then they left.

How do you explain heartbreak? How do you function after great loss? How do you walk, talk, eat, breathe? How do you live? I don't know. I must have done so. I must have. I think I sat on the lounge all night and tried to let the knowledge wash over me that Andrew was dead. I think I nearly got it once but searing pain twisted my heart and rescued me from the awful picture and I crawled back into that blessed relief called 'denial'. And I stayed in limbo for a very long time.

Sunday morning at exactly 10.00 am I was ushered into an icy room. The room was bare except for a long table which held my son's broken body. After 10 minutes with Andrew I left, but my heart and soul remained in that icy room.

I wrote Andrew a farewell letter and was determined to be strong enough to read it at his service. I stood tall and proud as I thanked my darling first born for his love and loyalty, dedication to his brothers and the many roles he played within our family, brother, father, mother, friend. I felt crucified with guilt.

I was aware of everything yet not really awake. I was in a drunken stupor; I knew what I did but didn't know why I did it.

Every room in my house protected me from the outside world. I peeped through the curtains looking for Andrew but refused to open the door when I heard knocking; I checked my phone for his messages then became terrified when the phone rang and was unable to answer it. I was completely crazy. I treasured the quiet time and, without realising what was taking place, I fell into severe depression and utter insanity. And I bargained endlessly with God for just one more hour, one more minute so I could say goodbye. God, I begged, 'Can you hear me God? Answer me God!' And I talked to my full glass of wine and to my tumbler of Scotch and to my case of beer. And to Andrew. And to no-one else.

All I wanted was Andrew and the rest of the world hurtled by me with heart-stopping slowness.

It is now 2019 and my heart is somewhat at peace however I will forever be a bird with a broken wing, a glass half full, an echo in a forest of hurt.

Grief
Leanne Pettigrew

Today I realised what true grief was

It isn't when the diagnosis is given. When there is a glimmer of hope. When prayer may still be answered.

It isn't when reality sets in and you realise that no matter what you do, there will be no happy ending.

It isn't when you try to cram as much living into each day as possible because you know there are less days to make memories that will sustain.

It isn't when you huddle around the bed and the moment you have dreaded has arrived—goodbye my darling.

It isn't the funeral when those who loved you as well, gather to say goodbye.

It isn't the ensuing days, weeks, months . . when friends cry with me. Stories and memories are shared. I am still safe.

I discovered true grief tonight . . . sitting around a table with new friends and none of them knew you . . . would never know you . . . and my heart broke completely.

Sadly now, I understand grief.

The Cartographer
Frances Lovell

I try to settle the brittle parchment of your skin
gently against
the bed sheets that skim the contours of your body.
My blunt, round fingertips seek to give you succour from
the deep, aching wells of pain.
I tell myself that it's comforting for you.
That my touch is good for you.
But it is for me, really.
For, to not be able to touch you,
ever again,
is unthinkable.
There is some solace to be found in the warmth
of the clots of sunlight
which froth the air through a window,
which cannot be opened.
I wish I could open it to let some life in.
I meant noise.
That would be a distraction.
Instead,
I exhale with the bold vividness of a gong echoing,
and brush your hair from your forehead.
To touch, your skin is cool and dry.
I am,
I suppose,
giving you a benediction of sorts.
Bleakly,
I fold in on myself, on the chair beside you.
Settling along my body's familiar creases.
You are fading.
Not lost.
Just leaving.
A map being redrawn.

Tears and the Sea
Julie Sladden

I found a lump. Sounds innocuous when you say it like that. It was about the size of a pea. Really, it was. Small. Hard. Painless. I was sitting watching telly with my boys and my hand was resting under my armpit as I massaged my sore muscles from the day's swim.

'Well, that's new,' I thought. My next thought was one of annoyance, 'What a pain in the arse.' As a doctor, I knew the next steps—the ultrasound, the mammogram (ouch), the needle biopsy—but ultimately it would need to come out. And it was probably benign. I had no family history of breast cancer, I was fit, healthy and young. Really, I had no risk factors for breast cancer. So, my ultimate feeling was one of annoyance, not alarm.

But it wasn't. And I'm on the conveyor-belt. I'm pushed, pulled, prodded. Parts of me are removed. I don't own myself anymore. Did I ever? All of a sudden it feels like everyone else has more 'weighin' on what happens to me next, than I do. There's a tidal-wave of cards and flowers and calls and messages. I can't keep up. I just want to leave. Escape from it all. Would anyone notice? I could leave the defective parts of me behind if that helps.

Then as quickly as it begins, it ends. The wave recedes back into the sea. Taking parts of me with it. I'm not sure what's left. And so I begin to swim again. The water soothes my battered body. My tears mix with the sea, and no-one can tell. Only the sea knows. Out there I can just be me. No one can get to me. And so the sea heals me.

Pearl Grey
Sara Crane

They say we disassociate to protect ourselves
from the savagery of traumatic events
in the quiet of 3ams on the way back from the city
we use to go to old Callum Park, find florescent algae in the water
our very own Life of Pi with take away food and cigarettes
no ghosts, only cops, drug dealers and lovers.

My hair went pearl grey the year I turned 35
unsure if the hairdresser meant to compliment me
when she described it so poetically
I used to be that deep brunette
like the many colours of tea that I drink.

There were moments after the storm passed
where I gurgled through self-doubt
days when my sieve of a head gushed
dry and I plugged the holes of my memory
I know they laughed at the post it notes
I stuck across my computer screen
they never cared that I tried to keep up
just that I didn't.

I am an imposter, a stranger in my own office
a loitering child in oversized clothes
I am a faded pair of jeans and cold coffee
the lost memo already shredded and I am sitting here
sticky taping myself back together; unreadable
Tv shows are now my box of chocolates, chocolate my new crutch
I am a plot line waiting for the hero's call to action
I've made friends with Arya Stark, Sookie Stackhouse and Offred.

They say we disassociate as a survival technique
that my meditation is so millennial
I slowly unpack the compressed and unspeakable events
I reconstruct brain cells one at a time and when I am ready
I will work on the appearance, take down the post it notes
maybe my brain will have plugged up all the holes in my head
and when it is time, they'll sit me down
explain to me why I didn't get the job
I will tell them I already know.

The Ones From Coles
Nalin Jeenmuang

5
whenever my siblings and i got sick, my father wouldn't let us eat; he said that our stomachs were weak and couldn't digest food properly. we were only allowed home-made juices and water. one day my aunt offered to look after me when i was sick and home from school. with my mum and dad at work, my aunt asked me if i was hungry and i nodded feverishly. she fed me rice with pork and my stomach felt great, i felt the sickness leaving me.

6
my dad became very sick when i was six and refused to eat any food. mum would cry and yell at him for not eating and he would always say he could only stomach home-made juices and water. when i told him about the time my aunty fed me pork and rice when i was sick and how it made my stomach feel he laughed and said that my stomach was much stronger than his. he said that his stomach was too weak to handle any of it, but i knew he was lying to himself.

6 ½
on the day of my father's funeral we had cheese and bacon rolls for breakfast, the ones you get from coles. i remember telling mum that maybe if dad had eaten some when he was sick, his stomach would've felt great and fought off the cancer. she cried and hugged me like she needed it more than i did. every new year's, christmas, easter, and on the 25th of april (my dad's birthday), my grandma brings my dad's favourite foods to his headstone and tells him to eat up. 'you're too skinny,' she'll say to him, 'you're all bone.' i'd whisper 'yeah dad' and pour a can of coke into a glass for him.

14
the day my mother was diagnosed with cancer she ate everything and anything she loved. she cooked up a feast and told us to eat as much as we wanted. when she went into surgery to remove the cancer, she requested that my aunt take us out to the grocery store to pick out anything we wanted to eat. i picked cheese and bacon rolls, the ones you get from coles, and left one in the plastic bag for my mum so that she could have it after she got out of the operating theatre.

16
when i was sixteen i worked at baker's delight. i had an abundance of free bacon and cheese rolls at my fingertips. i didn't touch them.

21
my mother has been cancer free for five years. whenever we go to the doctors for her annual check-up we stop to pick up a pack of cheese and bacon rolls, the ones you get from coles.

First day after
Pam Schindler

I brought you with me
that first morning—
you borrowed my face
to feel the sun

around us the butcherbird voices
in strained clarity
sang the heart of the day—
you were listening too

I counted first things
as they arrived without you—
I brought you a cloud, a bird
a slant of light,
offered them one by one

and then you gave them back:

the first moon, golden,
that you brought me with both arms

I didn't mean for you to die

Geoffrey Ahern

It's pouring down rain but I don't care. In fact, this is good. I deserve discomfort. I deserve to be punished. I deserve to feel even more pain than I'm currently feeling.

The rain is loud, there's thunder and the occasional flash of lightening. As I walk to my baby son's grave I'm thinking how poetic it would be if I was struck down by a lightning strike on his grave. Maybe this would be a form of justice.

I know his death wasn't really my fault. I did what I was told to do. It was four in the morning. I was exhausted. I was panicking. My wife was literally bleeding to death. But my baby son was desperately struggling for breath. I was completely out of my depth as the midwife frantically screamed directions at me so that I could save my dying baby while she saved my wife.

I look just above her head and there's an emergency button. Inside my head I'm screaming at myself to get up and press the button.

The midwife yells at me, 'We don't need help, we can do this on our own.'

But I knew we needed help. How the fuck does a young man with no training save a new born baby gasping for breath?

I'm down on my knees at his grave now. The rain is hitting my back so hard that it's like little electric shocks. I'm sobbing uncontrollably. And then I'm screaming; blood curdling screams from the depths of my soul.

'I'm so sorry. I'm so sorry. I didn't mean to hurt you. I didn't mean for you to die.'

How do you live with something like this? How do you recover when you've seen it written in black and white that you contributed to your own son's death? How do you forgive yourself? Can you even contemplate the idea of forgiveness? I hate the woman who placed me in this situation but I can extend forgiveness to her, not for her sake, but my own. But I can't extend the same grace towards myself.

I wonder if heaven really exists. And if it does, and if by chance I get there, will my son walk up to me and forgive me? Or will he run to me and hit me, screaming at me, demanding for me to explain why I let him die, why was I such a coward and why didn't I tell the midwife to get fucked. The coroner said my son would be alive if I did.

It's over 20 years later and I still feel guilty and ashamed. I feel like his death has been eating away at my insides like a slow growing cancer, and on my worst days I ask God to end my suffering and take me off this planet. But he doesn't. Maybe he wants me to suffer too?

But I'm still here. A lot worse for wear and still wondering what will happen when I die.

Father
Laura Jan Shore

His legs crumple
and I cushion his fall with my body,

the two of us sliding down the bathroom wall,

his bare legs skeletal, bluish bulbs
of reconstructed knees, stiff arthritic hands.

My modest father sits in the stink,
the colostomy bag split and spattered.

He's listing to the left. I stroke
the crepe paper skin of his once brawny arm.

I try not to gag, will my throat to relax.

Wordless, on the cold tiles, we
lean into each other.

He, who was everything—
vital and out of reach.

Inured to the stench, I suck in the rhythms
of his breath, the physics of death—

our stillness amidst the wreckage.

Hand Hygiene

Jeanette Lacey

'... I don't know why your sister took all your Mum's money... My priority is looking after your Mum. You won't get this opportunity to sit by her side, to be present, to honour this woman you call 'Mum' again. Perhaps try to focus on that?'

I close the door behind the grief. Leaving it in the room. Leaving the years of anger, mother-daughter dynamics, love, tough love ... tears. The notes are written, the words are careful, professional, in case they are read.

I turn, the nurses are busy, they don't stop: this man needs antibiotics, that lady a dressing, he's angry, she's frightened, 'when is the surgery?' I hear her companion ask.

The opportunity to perform my one minute of hand hygiene before I open the next door, *breathe in, breathe out, I'm doing my best, I let go of the rest, breathe in, breathe out.*

The emotion hits me, the exhaustion, pure unbridled agony fills the room. He looks awful, not long to go, she watches each agonising breath, he moves, she jumps. She might die too. 'He's my everything, he's too young, there's so much more to do' she spews forth the words and collapses into him again.

I sit, I watch. *Breathe in, breathe out.* He keeps going. I listen, I touch, his body sweats with the pressure of trying to do what it's done for 67 years, but knowing, it can't keep going.

She starts to talk to me. 'We went to the Territory'... the stories come, the memories, they flood from her, they don't stop, she talks and talks and talks. Only stopping to JUMP. He moves, 'what is it?' she says, 'nothing, I love you' his eyes roll back to check into his brain, *breathe in, breathe out.* She goes on. For a moment I'm lost in his breathing, she's lost in the memories. She brings me back with talk of ice cream. He loved ice cream. I love ice cream, the dying love ice cream, it's sweet and cold and delicious, and who can blame them? Have it for breakfast, why not, life is short.

She's still talking, she can't stop, if she does, she'll think—about her loss, her best friend, her husband, her career, her income, all gone, so much loss. Now she stops, he's stopped. She waits. We all wait... and wait. He starts again. She collapses into him, her eyes roll, she passes out.

I excuse myself after she recovers, 'I'll be back,' I promise. They hold me, they don't want to let go. The pain is too much to bear. I write my notes, it's hard to describe that pain.

The opportunity to perform my one minute of hand hygiene before I open the next door, *breathe in, breathe out, I'm doing my best, I let go of the rest, breathe in, breathe out.*

Meditation upon the passing of a day
Claire Wilson

You lay on a steel throne, lined with white sheets,
you made your ruling
'This is the last day I love you'
in truth,
no words,
you spoke through eyes weary
eyes done
what was theirs to do.
Late summer stopped.
Cockatoos came to take you away
Remains.
We tended the shell,
the crown,
the glory that was you

I wandered a wood, damp moss, and cracking sticks underfoot
in this the long-awaited dream of spring.
The inflorescences were very white—
blossoms burst from bony limbs
eyes down, I sought the undergrounds
but still they slept in their subterranean world
waiting for the days of the dying sun
when in a sudden fit they would throw forth
ineffable organs of sponge, gills, and spore.
But there and then in that young spring
last year's leaves fell from the trees.
Night came early on that day
but, a realisation, we are the ones spinning,
the sun is still there—making matter
into energy; radiance.

Heelys
Elizabeth Kuiper

When I was eight all I wanted was a pair of Heelys. These were essentially roller-skates but with one lone wheel located in the heel of the shoe. The adverts on TV featured teenagers skating through shopping malls in America, boasting about their 'rad new kicks'. Heelys soon became a regular feature on birthday and Christmas wish lists. When Dad got sick, Mum bought me a pair—blue with a white stripe. But that wasn't how I wanted to get them.

I learnt how to ride Heelys during the hospital visits. The smooth corridor floors were easy to slide along while the support-rails across the walls helped me balance. Around the corner from Dad's room was a set of parallel bars, the sort used for physical rehabilitation, which were perfect. I would rest my hands on either side and carefully propel myself forward, concentrating on the movement of my feet, while Mum was preoccupied by 'adult discussions'. I quickly became really good with my Heelys.

Mum told me I needed to say something at the funeral. I said that I didn't want to talk in front of a room of strangers.

'You like writing, don't you? You could write a poem,' she suggested. I told her that I exclusively wrote about magic talking bicycles and waking up with antlers on your head. But I wrote one anyway.

After his death, I trained my mind to barricade the memories. If I thought of what happened it was in a quick, rational way guided by necessity—checking little black boxes at the doctor's office, writing N/A under 'father's contact number' or declining an invitation to my high school's dad-and-daughter dinner dance.

It's been almost fifteen years. Grief does not permeate my day-to-day. But the milestones are tricky. Each of my major accomplishments in life—no matter how joyous—are made bittersweet, tempered by a constant question: what would he say if he were here? What sage advice may he have dispensed on my 18th birthday? How would he react upon hearing I got into law school? Or to me telling him I don't just write about talking bicycles anymore—that I'm about to have a book published? I'm not sure these thoughts will ever disappear. I imagine they'd persist if I were to pass the bar, or my Mum were to walk me down the wedding aisle. Or, even years later, as I spot a young child wearing a pair of Heelys.

[extract] A poem for Dad (2004)

My dad was very tall and thin
& I know I look a lot like him

From a story I made up
He used a character to name his pup

He used to sing Elvis songs
But often got the words all wrong

He spoke so many different languages
& at work always ate toasted chicken-mayo sandwiches

I love you Dad and always will
From your 'sausage'

Her Name is Sarahjane
Rebecca Gubalane

I spoke through disbelief and tears. The detective stood sheepishly behind me. The room fell silent but not for very long. Cue stage one of grief: Shock and Denial. A mess of hugs and red eyes erupted. I puked my insides up outside the police station. Tears and obscenities flew aimlessly. How can you feel everything and absolutely nothing at the same time? It scared the shit out of me. I sat there in the gutter. I saw her the night before. I said goodnight and left her at the pub with a smile and a drink in her hand. She was happy. I was happy. All the outside noise faded away while the noise in my head amplified. A rabid internal monologue. My sister's dead. What now? What next? My mind was tangled up in knots so tight I didn't know what to do. I lost myself that day. I left her sitting in that questioning room and I didn't even get to say goodbye.

I met my mother's eyes and it was if I suddenly had no bones. I was weak. A cannonball had hit our family and we all fell down. Two little boys had been left without a mother. Their pretty big brown eyes turned a sad shade of red and little droplets formed on the ends of their lashes. Those droplets turned into waterfalls as their faces changed. I remember it now and it still makes me sick to my fucking stomach. I can still hear their voices breaking. I remember their world changing. I remember my world changing. A darkness seeped into our skin and held my family hostage. Lifeless days passed. The children's father was charged with murder. A once-loved jilted nobody with an insidious plan. We packed up my sister's life and shoved it into boxes and spare rooms. Her silent home echoed. I came to find a strange comfort in my suffering. I had my very own safety blanket of melancholy.

My heart will forever have a hole in it. We lost her. Someone that once breathed in the same air we do. Someone who loved and hurt and cried like we do. She isn't just a name on the tip of sharp tongues. She isn't just old town gossip. She isn't just a newspaper headline for you to enjoy with your morning coffee. She was and still is my sister. We share the same eyes and olive skin. We share the same blood and flowing black hair and on that colourless day a piece of me died with her. She can't be here to watch her boys grow. To hear their tales of first kisses and battle their teenage angst. Her presence is only left for the imagination. What could have been and should have been has been stolen. I keep her alive tirelessly in my mind where she stays ageless and smiling. She is nowhere and she is everywhere. Her name is Sarahjane.

Before, During, After

Sueanne Gregg

We knew he was dying. The short trip from one side of town to another had been made. From home to hospital. 'A month,' the doctor had said. He was pretty close to it.

During that month there were more cups of tea drunk than any other time in my life. There'd be a knock at the door. 'We're here to see your dad.' 'Come in and have a cup of tea.' Another knock at the door.

During that month, people who had been part of our lives in the past came forward to say hello, say sorry, sorry goodbye. That they made the effort will always stay with me. Some of them we may never see again. It's just the way it is, and that's okay. And then there are those who were part of our 'now', but have disappeared. Sometimes it's too hard to stay, and that's okay too. And of course, those who were our 'now' and are still our 'now'. The best friends of all.

During that month, I lay beside my father on the bed he shared with my mother. 'I don't know what to say,' he said once. 'You don't have to say anything,' I answered. What can words say better than actions, really? A kiss on the cheek. Holding hands in silence. A cup of tea with friends.

During that month stories were told, jokes rolled off the tongue, a conversation of some sort always in the background. But always an undercurrent of sadness. It can't be completely forgotten. 'A month.'

When the time came, when my mother couldn't lift him to help him, we knew the decision had to be made. It was time to go to hospital.

When the time came, there was a new flurry of visitors. Family. Close friends. Final goodbyes.

When the time came, and his last breaths were taken, fresh tears flowed. But also for me, a feeling of lightness. His pain was gone. He didn't have to suffer anymore.

When the time came, it was too soon, it was too late. Two and a half short long years from diagnosis to death, and 'a month' of dying at the end.

Afterwards, the funeral.
Afterwards, inconsolable mourning.
Afterwards, the anger.
Afterwards, begrudged acceptance.
We knew he was dying. But it hadn't made it any easier.

Intensive Care
Lea McInerney

You are 24, I am 20. I sit on a chair at the foot of your bed, your nurse for the night shift. My job tonight though is not to save you. It's to watch over you as you die.

On the bench between us is a large sheet of paper, next to that, a pen. I look at the monitors above your head and write down the numbers. Your pulse and blood pressure, your temperature—very high and rising. It's not possible to remain alive much over this. I move to your side, ease open each of your eyes, shine my torch into them. I return to my seat and write 'fixed and dilated' once more.

You look fit, apart from not being able to breathe on your own. A machine does this for you, the bellows airing their robotic soundtrack through the room. 'Pfftt' every six seconds, pushing breath deep into your lungs, your chest rising and falling, going through the motions.

In the bed next to yours is an old woman. She's expected to make it. At her feet sits another nurse, the same age as me. We work together, help each other. Behind us in the windowed nurses' station, the senior staff watch on, ready to come if the monitors signal alarm.

Your people don't know yet. Strangers are trying to find them as I sit here with you.

The doctor tells me this is what happens sometimes with an overdose. That the drug's ability to alter you will continue, taking every perception you ever had with it, rolling you on, faster and faster, until it burns you out.

I go to the linen trolley and flick through the sheets, find the thinnest one, worn white cotton, lightest of touch on your skin. I dip a washcloth in cold water, squeeze it out and hold it to your brow, dab the corners of your closed eyes. I rinse the cloth and wrap each of your hands in its cool dampness. For your dry mouth, ice chips wrapped in gauze held softly against your lips.

I sit again at your feet and ask silent questions. What's happening deep inside you, to your spirit? When does it leave? Is this just your shell, or are you still all here, body and soul in a soundless struggle?

Finally your heart stops. The doctor disconnects you from the machine. We wash you, the other nurse and I, first your front, then I ease you over to your side, lean you against me, hold you steady while she sponges your back. Your skin is still hot. We talk quietly, sad for the loss, the waste, the parents, the brother, the sister, the lover, the others.

We wrap you in a shroud, secure it with pins. I go to the nurses' station, ring the orderlies, request a patient transfer to the morgue. Then I sit at your feet for the last time.

A wake for Amy

Kerry Harte

My father thought it weird to display
imprints of the baby's feet, captured
in plaster the day after her death, on
a cake guests would be offered to eat.

The tiny footprints my mother replicated
using soft icing the colour of cotton candy,
peeled carefully from each plaster cast, like
a band-aid from a new wound and placed

still warm from her kneading, to rest in
the centre of a heart shaped plaque
purchased from the cake-decorating shop
on our way from the hospital a lifetime ago.

My waiting father tapped the steering wheel,
as if marking time for a missile launch, until
a startled shop assistant came in search of help
to recover the sobbing woman collapsed

on the floor in the cake topper aisle. More bean
bag than blushing bride, he emptied her into
the car and we howled home like the ghost of
an emergency the ambulance failed to find.

Something I lost to the night
Cheryl Howard

I had bought a dress at the House of Merivale. I'd been in Melbourne a couple of months, having moved from Adelaide. It was 1972

The dress was olive green wool. It was the best I could afford, from the sale rack. I decided it would look better if I raised the hemline two centimetres.

I had plans. I was going to the Power House Dance overlooking Albert Park Lake.

That morning the young man whom I shared the kitchen with, asked me out.

I said no, telling him I had other plans.

Really, he was very nice, but I wasn't interested in nice. I was scared of nice. Nice might want to get close to me and I would panic, feel inadequate, fake.

It was hard for me to go off alone to places. I wasn't adventurous or confident.

I don't know what I expected to happen at the dance. If I met anyone who was interested in me, I wouldn't like them. Probably I hadn't at that stage fully understood that. Probably I thought that something mystical might transpire if the right person was there, that they could make it all right somehow.

When it ended I walked to the tram stop. A tram went past before I got there.

'That was the last one for the night.' It was a man's voice and he was right behind me. He caught up to me.

'Were you trying to catch that tram? I saw you at the dance.'

'Oh, it doesn't matter,' I said. 'I like walking.'

He asked me where I lived and pointed to his car parked just ahead and said he could easily give me a ride home.

He seemed so ordinary, kind; he'd seen a need and responded.

He asked me if I would like to have coffee. I felt that it would be rude to refuse. The café was at Abbotsford. Afterwards instead of doing a U-turn and heading back to my home he drove straight ahead, into Studley Park. I could just make out the dark sinuous river beneath us.

I had one thought only. 'I will survive this.'

I didn't want to be in Monday's newspaper: 'Unknown girl found dead in Yarra'.

I promised I wouldn't report the crime he'd just committed if he got me safely to the end of my street.

Driving back he ranted that it was my own fault, my dress was too short and so forth.

The sorrow that can't be spoken of becomes a grief like night. We go through our days but the hurt that is very deep has to work its way out.

After a week or so I thought I was okay because I stopped thinking about it. But really it was there all the time. Rape didn't cause my problems with intimacy but it most certainly compounded what was already there. Like a trap hidden in every interaction, just waiting to spring open and catch me.

The Whisper
Jannette Gibbons

Inside,

I want to lash out in a wild rage and punch and smash and batter my fists against bricks and mortar until my bones twist and crack and snap and my skin is torn away and my flesh is bleeding and raw and exposed. I want to slam my skull into concrete and blind my vision with dizziness and pound my head with throbbing to expel the vicious demons taunting me with ripped out pieces of my shattered heart, mocking me for bringing you into a world in which you could not flourish and thrive. I want the hollow ache engulfing my stomach and turning it into a churning pit of nausea and despair to swallow me up and spew me back out to fight the brutal and cruel reality savaging me to my core that I can do nothing to help you. I want to scream so loudly and violently that this pain and injustice finally reaches its crescendo and windows break and traffic stops and people pause and the sun blinks out and time stills and the entire universe knows what is happening.

Outside,

I hold your tiny body in my arms and whisper goodbye as you take your last breath.

No One Told Me That Grief Would Last My Entire Life
Claire J. Harris

25 years of dreams about my father
    I dreamed about my father last night. It was a dream I know well: the one where he shows up at our family home to explain that he has been alive all along, and there is a very simple reason why he couldn't come back to us sooner.

    My father died a quarter of a century ago—so, as the years go by, the explanations become less and less believable, the family home changes, and my dream father grows older. But the dream remains. The glimmer of hope has long since faded with his memories, but still the dreams come.

    I first had this dream a few days after my father's funeral—and I never imagined it would continue to haunt me decades later. There are so many things about grief that no one told me.

    I didn't know you could grieve for someone your entire life, even though you were only 11 years old when they died. No one tells you that this grief can surface again when you become an adult, thrusting you into a deep depression. Or that the sudden scent of a marker pen that smells like his office can hit you like a sucker punch to the stomach.

    No one tells you that the day when the amount of time you have spent without him surpasses the amount of time you spent with him is a terribly sad day. No one warns you that you can suddenly cry for the person you lost years ago as though it was yesterday.

    No one tells you that twenty years after your father has died, when you have to attend a funeral of someone else's father, you will collapse in tears at the sight of the coffin. Your friends might not think to accompany you to this funeral, because no one told *them* that you're still in lifelong grief and funerals will always be unbearable.

    No one tells you that you will feel the pangs of loss every time you travel—because your Dad travelled the world when he was the same age as you and you just wish you could tell him about it. No one says anything about the imaginary conversations you'll have with him in your head, year in and year out, as you follow in his footsteps and try to see the world through his eyes.

    You don't know yet that you will become obsessed with tracking down people who knew him in remote countries. Or that when the search proves fruitless, you will grieve all over again for all the missing pieces of the puzzle that you'll never be able to fit together.

    No one tells you that the words 'My father died when I was a child' will gradually become less difficult to say out loud, but will never ever be painless.

    And no one tells you about 25 years of dreams.

Light
Carmel Macdonald Grahame

I remember apricot light on the horizon,
pulling darkness into it. And of all things, blood,
how it streams from my brother's swing-hit temple,
congeals in the corner-shop storyteller's shark-tale ring,
stains my mother's skirt with far-fetched secrets,
is thicker than water—words that freeze love
on my mother's tongue and leave it
there, for safe-keeping.

I remember the relief of after-school light in a kitchen.
This time my mother is sewing pyjamas,
for me, a daffodil muslin-and-lace concoction
she has been fitting on my little brother until I come in.
His eyes follow yellow thread trundling into stitches,
and when his dress turns out to be mine, he is inconsolable—
all that wading ankle-deep in a pool of frills,
stoic scissor-holding, pin-scratched standing still—

I will never forget us snaps-and-snailing him
and puppy-dog-tailing him into his boys-own-only life.
Or the hole in the world he left—
it appears now as shy constables with dangling hands
filling the kitchen talk with gravel roads, a ditch,
becomes a chapelful of candle shadow, turns
into a rectangle, too cutout-clean in orange sand.
It ends there, in deciduous light being shed on grief.

Love Hurts
Caroline Freedman

Christine studied the array of tattoos on Lindsay's right arm. Generally she hated tattoos—she thought they were tacky. The one that stood out to her the most was the Gingerbread Man. She wondered how much money these tattoos had cost Lindsay over the years and why she'd chosen to cover her arms in such a way.

Christine stroked the outline of the Gingerbread man lovingly and felt the warmth of her sister's soft skin. Lindsay's long red hair was pulled back from her face, falling about her right shoulder. The dusty clock on the wall ticked in unison with the breathing apparatus that was keeping her alive.

The acrid taste of vomit formed a crust in Christine's mouth and her eyes were battered with her sobbing. The nurse in the corner respectively went about his business; Christine had forgotten he was there. His name was Ryan, a coincidence; their brother's name was Ryan, he would arrive on the first flight of the morning from Newcastle.

Christine adoringly surveyed every aspect of her sister—tracing each of her fingers, touching the silver ring that was cutting off the circulation of her right index finger. She looked so beautiful; so alive. Her chest was rising and lowering underneath the obligatory crisp white hospital sheet, and she felt wonderfully warm to touch. Ageing had not ravaged her, yet. Whilst Christine played with the cheap ring on her sister's finger she felt her sister squeeze her hand. It was wishful thinking; an involuntary twitch, the doctors said it was catastrophic, she reminded herself.

Christine chatted away to her sister, recalling childhood memories, Irish dancing competitions and then begging her to wake up and not leave her, not leave her kids. She fluctuated between grief and utter disbelief to the foreboding realisation of her situation.

Nurse Ryan shuffled about taking observations. He talks to Lindsay, informing her of the process he's about to take. He does this more for Christine's sake though. An eerie yellow beam breaks through the dirty venetian blinds signalling daybreak. Christine breathes in deeply and braces herself for the day that's about to come—a day she must face as the one in which she loses her beloved little sister.

She kisses Lindsay's warm wrinkle free forehead, and strokes her luscious long red hair for the last time ever; turns her back and prepares herself to tell Lindsay's seven year old son that there'll be no Mother's Day today.

Half-Life
Denise

During my days, I paint-by-numbers through my life and function on some level. But in the black of night, wide awake and fretful, I take my son's story in my hands. I prod it and poke it and shake it like a rag doll in the hope the truth will fall out. But truth does not fall out of the mouth of an ice addict. Let alone an ice addict charged with child pornography charges. His tale is a pantomime of lies, half-truths, omissions, embellishments, fabrications. And he handed it to me in some desperate attempt to have me believe it. And of course I couldn't. Now he won't talk to me or see me. I did not agree to his desperate request for thousands of dollars for a barrister. So I'm no use to him. A million questions crawl around my brain and I have no means to access answers. How serious are these charges? Will he go to jail? How did it come to this? I feel revulsion and rage that a child of mine would partake in such a vile industry, harming children. And on top of all this, I miss him terribly.

Jon was a blond-haired, affectionate little boy. I adored him. His big sisters did too. He was their little toy; funny, sweet and generous. Of course, I blame myself for ending my marriage when he was seven and for the acrimony between me and his dad which had a deep and lasting effect on him. Jon felt torn, lost, and angry. My sister, my one confidante of this shameful story, forbids me to feel guilty or responsible for Jon's choices. But I wear it all the same, a tattoo of guilt on my forehead.

I live like a hermit. My friends know nothing. I cannot trust myself to be with them. I cannot sit at coffee shops and listen to updates on their successful sons. Those who've become fathers, with careers and kids and homes. I cannot form answers to any questions about Jon. So I stay home and attack the vegetable garden with fury.

It was his birthday last week. I had not seen him for over a year. I agonised over what to do. In the end I baked a cake and dropped it on his doorstep. Not even sure if he is living there still. Not sure it was safe from dogs. Not sure if he'd get it. Or want it. I received no response.

My son lives less than an hour's drive from me yet is lost to me. I grieve every day for what he could have been and what he has lost. The road back for him is incredibly long, and I don't see him navigating this. The family speaks in absolutes: 'He will never again see my children . . . .' and 'I will have nothing further to do with . . . .'

And me, I stand in the middle: living a half-life, adrift and broken.

Teacher
Niko Campbell-Ellis

The bell rings and they tumble in, chattering like birds. I gather them into a circle on the mat and, soon, too soon, the time has come.

I clear my throat. It's dry, it hurts to swallow, the words I have to say are shards of glass in my oesophagus. This morning's staff meeting sits heavy in my mind. The impossible instruction to 'try not to scare them,' the way my stomach dropped to the floor.

'I want to talk to you all about something that happened in New Zealand on Friday.'

Eyes, brown, blue, green, grey, look at me. Most are bright, trusting, no clouds shade their sunny skies. How can I say this? How can I lay the darkness of the world at these small feet?

But I do. Because the principal said we had to. Because 'something has to come from us and too much is being said out there'. Because 'out there' is the playground and this town and their phones and the whole world. Because maybe I can soften the blow.

Teacher. What a thing to teach. I swallow the broken glass, take them by the hand and lead them down a path of pain and grief. I tell them, as gently as I can, that 50 people who were praying peacefully are now dead at the hands of a man who hated them for nothing they did but everything he'd been taught they stood for.

I try to lead them in a way that keeps their love of the world intact. I try to put as few dents as possible in their trust of people.

I try to tell the truth, even though it's hard.

'Why does the man hate Muslims?'

'Because he doesn't understand them, and not understanding made him scared.'

'But why did he kill them?'

'I don't know. I don't think anyone can understand why he did that.'

But when Ruby asks if people hate her because of what she believes, I am choked by the truth. How is it that I live in a world where there are people, adults, who hate this little girl because of the religion she was born into? How is it that there are adults who would kill her for that hate?

My eyes spill over, mirroring Ruby's. Our tears spread like a virus. They slide down noses, are wiped on sleeves, are sniffed up. Tissues are handed around the circle. Fingers stretch and wrap around one another like tendrils, as the children, even those who would normally shun such contact, try to hold themselves afloat on a raft made of each other's warmth. I try to let this spontaneous display of kindness buoy me but Ruby's question is rocks in my pockets. I think I will drown.

    I tell Ruby that anyone who has ever met her knows she is a kind and lovely person.

    'But what about people who don't know me?'

    And the children all lean in, waiting for an answer.

Interior Castle
Ann-Marie Blanchard

for Karna

I live in a house where bodies slop drugs.
I live in a house where a woman turns blue.

Jude is in seizures, hand a banana smash;
Aggie's melting her mum's gold again.

Mary knocks and baby kicks.
Mary's got gear and baby wisdom.

I'm codeine coddled (for baby)
but I dream of heroin: dandelion

fat, spider sack. Dad drowned
baby mice. Said, don't tell.

Dad touched me. Said, don't tell.
Home explodes with dying beings:

bathtubbloatedbluegirlpurple.
Mary tightens the tourniquet.

This'll make baby strong—

Letting Go
Trish Bolton

Laura loops the twine between her fingers, secures her life with a neat bow.

Bank statements, tax file numbers, passwords. Wills. She has thought about this day for weeks. Planned and prepared. But still she has not found peace.

Venturing outside, she braves the icy wind. Somewhere there is snow. The cold stings and goosebumps rise on her arms. She steps off the verandah, feels the rush of wind across her face, the mess it's making of her hair.

Back inside, she eases herself into a favourite chair, the spike of pain a reminder her medication is almost due. Her legs are heavy, her once slender ankles fat with fluid, and there's a tiredness she's never felt before. She hears Jeremy wandering up and down the stairs looking for her. She is sure he senses something.

Laura hated taking away his last little piece of independence, trusting him somehow when he promised never to go beyond the front gate. When his wanderings grew more frequent, she had a handyman add a snib, sure it would bamboozle him and be much too high to reach.

One day he wasn't bamboozled and he did reach.

He had been gone twelve hours when police found him beside a busy highway, arms wrapped around his knees, rocking and weeping and calling her name.

She hopes not to be judged too harshly.

Not by her children. And not by Clare.

Clare, her oldest and dearest friend, the only person she might have told. Clare, no matter how distraught, would keep her secret. When they had kissed goodbye after meeting for coffee—how long ago last Tuesday seemed—Laura clung to her, almost giving herself away. She hurried off, waving goodbyes and agreeing to catch up in a week or two.

She walks through the door and closes it without looking back.

Laura guides Jeremy to the bathroom, helps him pull down his track pants, removing his pad as she nudges him onto the seat. She looks down at his still thick head of hair, feels, as she so often does, a great surge of tenderness. Their life together has not been perfect. But he loved her in spite of her failings, and she, mostly, loved him back.

Catching her reflection in the mirror, she sees a face crumpled into insignificance, the once determined jaw dissolving into the concertinaed folds of her neck, only her eyes, if looked at closely, bear witness to her wit and intellect.

Gripped by a moment of doubt, she trembles, then catches herself.

There can be no going back.

Laura organises a glass of wine to toast their lives together. She goes through the CDs choosing Jeremy's favourite. Whenever she teased him about his daggy taste in music he would laugh and waltz her around the room.

Jeremy opens his arms wide.

Soon they will go to bed, bodies and lives entwined.

But now, they will dance.

On Love
Paige Duffy

Early-morning light, that soft glow that's not quite daytime, curls around the edge of the blind, reflecting off the white material so the room while dimly lit is easily discernible. Looking at the light, that glow, I reach for my phone on the nightstand, and my metal water bottle reverberates off the floor as I do. My wife groans. Just after six. And a missed call from my mother with a text message stating to call her.

'Who died?' my wife remarks from somewhere beneath the green-and-white-striped doona, the cheap polyester clinging to her face, as I read aloud. I huff in response, a smile on my lips, and punch redial.

'Hey, mamma. How's things?' We talk of nothing. Satisfied, I go to say goodbye, but she tells me to wait. There's just one more thing.

'Honey,' she exhales, 'grandpa died.' I smooth the doona over my legs.
'Hello?'
'Yeah.'
'He passed this morning.' A magpie calls outside.
'I can't come back,' I say.
'I know. And grandma doesn't want you to either.'
'Are you sure?'
'It's too expensive.'

My mother tells me goodbye; I hold my thumb to the screen longer than it takes for the call to end. I think of my grandmother, her soft eyes, crinkling at the edges when she smiles, the way her lips pull tight when she smiles, severe yet warm. I think of her grief, three thousand kilometres away. My wife, beside me, falls asleep again, the green and white polyester pulled back over her mouth where soft snores escape, and I think of my grandfather, my grandmother's husband, dead in a crisp, clean hospital bed. The air-conditioner breathes.

When my grandfather smiled, his mouth pulled back and parted, revealing his too-big teeth without restraint. He smiled a lot; I always remember him smiling. In my bed, so far from my memories of him, my mouth burns as it did when my grandfather made hot cocoa the way I hated, when he left, as he always did, the skin of the milk on top. I think of the teacher he was, not only to strangers but to my own classmates, to me. The knowledge he had and the knowledge he shared, and how the knowledge crumbled along with his neocortex.

I have a photo of a stranger saved on my phone, the last photo my grandmother sent me of her husband. I see a frail man, an empty man, sitting in a plastic chair at a plastic dining table in a room of plastic. His eyes don't meet the camera. His mouth hangs open. He wears a red Christmas hat with red

and green bells sewn into the white rim.
    At two-thirty-two that Saturday afternoon, I think of my grandmother three thousand kilometres away, of her husband, and of my wife. Tears well in my eyes and fall. They will not stop. And I clutch my stomach, holding the parts of me together.

In That Desperate Hour
Katheen Kituai

For George Ingham, a carpenter, 1940 – 2003

I came across you
after someone had returned
        your chisel hammer saw
        to shadows on the wall
    hung instead, your penciled drawings
    Woodworks gallery, Bungendore

You'll never know that we met
or even promised to be there
        yet you understood me
        better than I understood myself
    I grasp this in your images
    of cushions hens cat

in the sort of pastels
you fell into
        when there were fewer afternoons
        than ways to get through them
    or avenues to explain
    what urges a carpenter, turned artist, to leave his mark

in that desperate hour before nightfall
                amid such pain.

My Sister
Robyn Moriconi

When my sister was born I was elated. I was the 17 year old eldest only daughter. After 4 brothers, to get a sister was the best present my parents ever gave me. I changed her nappies willingly, helped feed and wind her, devoted myself to caring for her as big sister, second only to Mum. As the youngest she was most spoiled and our mum's favourite, but I didn't mind.

Through the years we grew closer, drifted apart, closer again. Like an elastic band the bond was always there, even when we didn't agree, even when we were in different countries. My first child was born when she was 3; the practice I had with her was very handy then. She was close to my children, they grew up together like siblings and I was glad.

She grew into a troubled teen but overcame that. Our mother died when she was barely 21 and this shocked us all. My sister took a while to process her loss, veering off the rails again before her grief was supplanted by new life. She was a devoted mother, reliable friend, a rock and a butt kicker when the need arose. Nothing got past her, nothing fazed her, nothing kept her down . . .

But then she got sick. Tests and scans and tests and hospitals and scans and all the while she was the strong one, reassuring us that everything would be fine. Everything wasn't.

Shades of gray turned yellow, foreign colours adorned her body as the toxins macabrely claimed her. Yet she smiled constantly, downplayed her symptoms, stocked up on pineapple, kale, cannabis oil, vitamin boosts to stay well as she fought, in her usual style, to win. Tests, scans, hospitals, scans, radiation, chemotherapy. She kept smiling but we saw the grimaces increasing. Surgery bought her more time, her daughter's 21st birthday bash was a blast. We relaxed a little, she was winning.

Then came the call that revealed the truth. She was losing the battle and wanted to surrender on home soil. She had 2 weeks. She was 48 years old.

When my sister was dying I was devastated. I was 17 years older than her. I flew a few thousand miles to her side. I changed her nappies willingly, I held her hand, cried with her, fed and winded her, laughed and reminisced. I devoted myself to caring for her, spoiled her, as did my brothers, but we didn't mind. Fences were mended, goodbyes said. I dressed what was left of her and they took her shell away.

It should have been me.

The Persistence of the Image
Damen O'Brien

Three years after she left us, my youngest wakes
crying and cannot be settled—*it's not fair*—
and I have loose threads to console him, flakes
garnered from pop psychology. I share

poor blank verse substitutes for purpose,
cheap and cheerless platitudes for death.
He plunges back through sleep's fragile surface:
the other frontier of the empty breath.

Strange congruencies and triggers: I'm reminded
out of the blur of memory, of my Grandmother,
long after her death. So how may I find
an answer to the eternal persistence of love?

His memories are as an image made in water:
when the maker walks away, the light persists;
in that supple rubber curve, the surface supports
a reliquary for light which fades, but life insists

on recollection, on ripples at the surface, a lash
length of the eye. He wails somewhere in the night,
and I rise to soothe him, with my memories, a flash
as wide and deep as water but more bright.

Not Scared of Flying
CJ Vallis

Hot breath in my ear, 'Are you sure?'

Maybe. I'm at least a dozen beers past caring. It's my eighteenth birthday and Nan can't stop me. Party songs blare down the hall—*boogie funk groove*—throbbing like headaches.

His cement weight pours, sinks my body in mattress. Deep in concrete dream, I slip. Let go.

I'm eight. My school perches high on a slope. You could say it's my runway. Downhill, I run. Faster, faster. My arms spread, I leap and soar. For dizzy seconds, I am weightless. Airborne.

I try to fly, far away.

Fail.

School kids mock my flapping wings. 'Loser,' they yell.

I hop away, feathers ruffled. Walking home, I pick jasmine, its sap and scent soaking into my hands. I squint at blue sky, at clouds blowing across strange dreams. Where does sky start and stop, and where am I to go?

The man-on-me reaches under my bra and rub-rubs. Like a boy scout willing sparks from the friction of dry nipples.

'You like that?'

I think I croak, 'Yeah.'

The fire reminds me of Cynthia, who lived next door. Together we were lemonade, Nan said, *very sweet*. I was lemon, Cynthia sugar.

I wish Cynthia knew the man-on-me. Cynthia was my Girl Guide. We played 'survival.' We stuck plasticine and strawberry food colouring to Barbie dolls to fake bloody injuries. Bandaged broken heads.

My eyelids flutter open. Did I invite man-on-me to my nest? Maybe. His stubbly face is in shadow. He reeks of beer. Eyes shut again—I have a dream to forage through and memory to scavenge.

The man-on-me tugs at my jeans. He jokes, 'Could they be any tighter?'

Jokes.

I want my nan. Cynthia would do.

Instead I've been left with Nan's house. The date palm outside my bedroom window, its sharp fronds and just-for-show fruit.

Better than flowers on Cynthia's coffin. She would've hated white roses and sprays of baby's breath, wilting in the heat. Years ago now. Nan only recently stopped living because she figured I could look after myself.

I could.

In this dream, my concrete legs are dragged apart to the noise of another pounding dance track—*sexy crazy lady*. Outside a flock of voices compete to be heard, honking laughter.

Who are you? I bawl to myself.

Cynthia would find out. She'd locate me with a compass or by the stars. Answer with an oath, a tricky knot and smoke signal.

Unlike Nan who'd shake her head, *I told you parties won't make you popular. What are you going to do now?*

He punctures thin lemon skin, 'Oh!'

Citric acid-juice.

Now what will I do?

Not what you think.

I'll shuck the lemon. Dream off the man. His desire is not cemented in me. I run in reverse, beyond nipple fire, past date palms, sweet-smelling jasmine and back up the school slope.

Am I scared? Maybe.

The sky waits. Soon I will fly.

And I'll never tell Nan or Cynthia or you.

How Not to Kill People (Notes)
Cassandra Scott

February. Sit, try not to think of his conversations with her. Open your book. Three paragraphs. Close. Distraction never slows the creative mind. Your thoughts without control begin to invent reality at speeds which makes you dizzy and confused.

Move from the couch to check messages from him only to discover there are none. Imagine them meeting in expensive restaurants: places with luxurious linen tablecloths and waiters that hover nearby carrying elegant pepper grinders. The meals resemble abstract art rather than food. He orders her two desserts because she can't choose.

Get jealous. Break your phone.

When he arrives at the apartment you talk only about music.

Talking becomes an exercise in observation and prediction. As you draw in the margins of notebooks you consider befriending a writer. Of course it's a stupid idea: he is a writer.

March. Raindrops rush down the window held up against the night-time world of the street. The barrier makes little difference as cold wet air presses itself into the room, into your flesh and bones. Sit drenched and emotion-soaked staring at walls.

This is how you pretend you're alive: by looking at things.

Express dislike towards other women. Make lists of girls you don't like: ones in love, ones who lie, ones who don't respect other women. Feel worse somehow. Question your morals. Look up articles on relationships and conclude those writers are, in fact, single.

The front door slams.

'We can't afford to go out,' he says. You sigh quietly but he notices.

'Next month I'll take you to that place across town you like to walk past.'

'Sounds good,' you say. Begin copying his visa card bills in secret.

April. Attend a party at his friend's house. It is an old house with small rooms that smell of damp moss. Assume the safe position next to the snack table viciously biting into carrot sticks—the crunching sound as your teeth split the solid vegetable mass is almost as satisfying as breaking his neck.

Think of how this helps both physical and mental health.

'You're turning into a rabbit,' he jokes. Amusing his friends is a priority. You tell him how often rabbits have sex and watch his expression become uncomfortable. Say you need a cigarette and leave.

You haven't smoked since '94.

Wait for him to stop you; walk home alone.

August. Swear using made up words like 'fucktard'. Be silently amused by your creative genius until he starts to cry. Stare at the cluttered kitchen bench that rests between you both: a quiet island, a silent third party trying to stop the fight by occupying the space between. The unorganised mess of the apartment acts like magnets, drawing together more debris from surrounding areas.

You haven't cleaned in weeks, your mind on vacation somewhere always sunny.

He says, 'I just want to love you'.

You cry. Thoughts slow, refusing to turn.

The door clips shut.

Sit, try not to think.

The Window Across the Way
Kristen Roberts

In the window across the way
the cord of the blind is swinging,
its arc already narrowing
behind the rain-spattered pane.
Every morning I miss the hand
that sets the cord in its metronomic sway,
miss the face that must surely measure dawn's breadth
as mine does each day,
and yet I remain incurious—
there's the tacit concord of city living
that we let the rain narrate the distance between us,
but also the immutable knowing
that it could never be you.

Now the Other One
Sharryn Ryan

Every Saturday morning, Dad and I would get into The Holden, and go and get Mum at The Salon, where she was having The Beehive done. By the time we arrived the chemical pall inside The Salon had been building for hours. The soup of it seemed to add heft to the air lock between the double front doors of The Salon, necessary to protect innocent pedestrians as they made their way unknowingly past the entrance outside. My father really had to put his shoulder into it to push his way inside.

During the weeks, when Dad came home, we'd be lined up in front of him. I could never remember what it was that we had done, but sometimes we'd been swinging on the clothesline.

Whatever it was, Mum had been prepping us for hours about our father's eventual arrival—'wait 'til your father gets home.' Then he'd appear, work things ringing in his head, while the sins and misdemeanours of the under 10's were spelt out in detail. As he listened to Mum, Dad would take off the leather belt from his suit pants. He'd hold it with his right hand, striking it menacingly against his leg, an evil black thing hissing and struggling to escape his grip. His face flushed with frustration and fury on those days, his eyes were black pitiless spaces burning out of his head. Our disciplining was fitted in between the second job, a part-time university course and his Catholic meetings. He was too tired, so not interested in our list of sins.

Sometimes it went too far even for Mum. She'd stand between our father and us holding her arms up dramatically, just like her favourite actresses did in the movies.

'No, Laurie, no. Stop it Laurie. That's enough.' She could be the hero then. But Dad was just getting started.

'Hold out your hand,' he'd say grimly when he was ready. He brought the belt down with all his strength. After a minute or two he got into the rhythm: 'now the other one' he'd repeat as he went from hand to hand and child to child, really putting his shoulder into it, just like at The Salon.

Dad never said anything about Mum's mental illness, or even admitted it existed. Maybe he thought if you don't talk about it you could make it go away. All he had in his tool-bag was that he was the good Catholic husband. All those feelings that didn't fit. He somehow managed his two lives never knowing that we could have been his allies, that we could have worked together. But we were just collateral damage in our parent's proxy war.

All except the youngest, David, nicknamed Piglet. Whatever happened, after David was born, it all stopped. Maybe Dad was exhausted, or maybe he couldn't bring himself to hit a little boy called Piglet.

Epithelial
Rose Lucas

cell by cell
the sheerest film creeps across
this open wound,
its jagged edges
its unthinkable territory;

    cell by cell and still
something grows even
    while I'm sleeping or
distracted or
disbelieving—

    neither with my will nor
    without it
something imagines a new surface,
 reach by branching
 reach—

as vulnerable as petals in spring rain;

as tender as the memory of
your face—

    you were looking down,
you were turning away from the light.

Tram 86

Kirsten Krauth

(for Aiia)

A sunflower bought at half price.
I join the wall of silence.
Hands in prayer positions.
A reporter crosses live.
Her face, heavy with makeup.
Her feet in thongs hidden from viewers.
A dog, whose job it is to be stroked.
Even when I'm wordless and I don't want it.

An aspiring rapper.
He steals words from this city.
I sit where you do, head turned.
My mouth and eyes closed, sleep missing.
A woman claims opera.
Her voice cocoons me.
From the bitter taste, of everyday conversation.
Wilting fast, I hold on.

The tram doors open.
Red roses, wrapped in plastic.
Your dad carries one posey, he chooses yellow.
A single iris sets my friend off.
Garden posies fresh, perfumed piles.
That fall while I catch them.
Head high to a small girl.
Wearing daisies and sandals.

The candles start to shudder.
As night takes you over.
The darkness stretches out, reflecting.
Mirrored gazes, dazed spaces.
I move on while your friends wave.
The same look on their faces.
Not seeing stars now, only black holes.
But still searching, beyond the streetlights.
To catch the ghost of you passing.

Time Crept By
Sophia Moore

July was icy, and the old cottages didn't hold their warmth. Darkness opened its jaw and engulfed the best parts of me. Splodge explained the phenomenon, but he left me with more questions. The questions tied a rope around my ankles and bedframe. I couldn't grace the day when the world seemed so bitterly cold.

When I walked down High Street, I saw familiar faces. The faces smiled and talked a lot. I vomited something verbally comprehensible. Sometimes the faces kissed me, and I'd wipe slobber off my cheek as we parted ways. When I felt suffocated by faces, I built walls with my blank stare.

Come summer, a woman I loved sat me down at Third Wheel Café. She said free love was not for her after all. And she had met someone wonderful. I wore a yellow jumpsuit to their wedding. I brought them gifts and buried my grief. My grief is still in a box under their tomato patch. I want to dig it up, but I hate making a mess.

Yellow shirts poured cement over the shore. They turned it into a basketball court. They said it was for the kids. As though the kids themselves had marched the streets, fists in the air, demanding the grass die.

Three years passed. And I never told my roof that I considered leaving. Because it was just an idea. And I didn't want my roof to worry. But in the middle of the night, I researched cheap flights. Just to feel like the door was ajar

On the Nature of Black Holes
Ruth Gilmour

Is it really nearly May?

Nearly 8 months then. 7 months and 24 days. If I'm being exact. Not that I'm keeping track.

I am keeping track.

6 years and 3 months since the girls in my dorm strung tampons dipped in red paint above my bed because I was the only one in our grade who hadn't got her period. And that made me weird apparently. 5 years, 6 months and 10 days since I began hormone replacement to 'jumpstart' my body and all that jumpstarted was a barrage of mood swings and migraines. 2 years and 2 months since the doctor looked at a chart, clicked her tongue, and said 'It doesn't look great . . . .'

7 months and 24 days since a blurry ultrasound screen finally confirmed that my ovaries don't produce eggs.

Loss makes sense. You have something, then it's gone. But how do I mourn an absence? How can I miss something I never had?

When I go out for coffee with Gran and she not-so-subtly hints at future great grandkids, what should I say? When I see a Mum with a pram walking down the street, sipping her latte and complaining to a friend about her 'crotch-fruit', how should I feel? When the Pilates instructor asks if anyone is injured or pregnant so she can modify the workouts accordingly and she looks directly at me with an expectant smile because I'm the youngest woman in the class and it makes logical sense that I'm the most likely to get knocked up, how should I react?

I attempt to arrange my face into something inoffensive and acceptable. Flippant exasperation, maybe? Accommodating wryness, perhaps?

Rampant anger?

Sometimes I imagine ripping her Pilates-perfect ponytail from her scalp. I imagine throwing things at Gran and slamming doors and bawling my eyes out. I imagine stealing babies from prams—'sorry, that's my crotch-fruit now'—and screaming and screaming until this emptiness goes away.

But I can't be one of 'those women'. Those women who make scenes and stamp their feet and wear their emotions like a medal. I must be socially palatable. People mustn't think I'm 'too much.' So I smile; amused, nonchalant, all of that, as beneath my skin and botched ovaries something primal, something of Genesis, of the dawn of time, makes me unravel. Kicks me right in the gut.

They found a black hole the other day. It's surreal, thinking that I was alive for one of those big historical moments. The photograph that popped up on my News page wasn't very impressive to be honest. A region of spacetime with a gravitational field so intense that no matter or radiation can escape condensed down to a fuzzy, orange spot. And darkness. And emptiness.

7 months and 24 days since the last blurry ultrasound. Another fuzzy spot. Another abyss that will never let anything in or out, that will never nurture, never cherish.

And darkness. And emptiness.

Sa tiyán ng lupà
Ivy Alvarez

My friends tell me to cry
grief is healthy
like exercise
or lentils

rivulets weave their way
down my face
trace its topography
salty tidal marks on my neck

where I used to like you
to kiss and bite
I bury my words
disguise my longing

for a non-existent past
work the heart muscle hard
it will not break
they tell me it will not

Filipino idiom meaning grave (literally, in the belly of the earth)

The Room
Sarah Pye

Time doesn't exist here: the light from the crack in the bathroom door seeps in like the first rays of dawn, throwing our internal clocks into jet-lagged confusion. The constant shuffle of feet and anxious buzzers are reminiscent of an airport and, I suppose, The Room is a similar waypoint on a personal journey. Nothing outside this building seems to matter. Newspapers, once cherished, no longer hold interest. Work is something to endure and rush back.

It's a place where visitors are welcomed during daylight hours and family covers every possible floor tile at night like refugees hoping for a better life. It's a vigil without a definite end. Like a roller coaster, (yet not in unison), our emotions rise and fall. The screams are buried deep inside.

At times the wait is interminable. At others we grasp every precious moment. Propped high on his white sheets and turned regularly, he wheezes as if snoring. Together we hold our breath as he labours his own. The tubes have been removed and we wait for his organs to go on strike. Five days after his last meal, they must be starting to protest.

'They wouldn't put a dog through this,' she whispers in a moment of panic. I squeeze her hand in agreement . . . it would be far easier if the doctors risked no incrimination by helping it along. 'You won't win this tennis match,' his son tells him, only partly in jest before whispering in his ear, giving him permission to leave.

It's as if emotions are no longer buried deep within our hearts, but spread, instead, in a thin layer over our skin. The simplest brush against another's feelings sends shock waves—intensely heart-warming and deeply disturbing. Barriers are down, conversations less guarded.

She talks about what it was like to meet him and how sexy he looked in rugby shorts. 'Sometimes I want to scream out to the nurses: *don't you know what this man has done?*' she says. I wonder if she is referring to his sporting achievements or his effect on her own heart. Together they have pushed and goaded each other into achieving more than they might have done alone.

Alone. On the first day it was not far from her mind. The thought of going home to an empty house instantly raised her blood pressure, moistening her eyes. Yet now, four nights later, some of the grieving has already taken place—words like 'lonely' and 'empty' gradually replaced with 'adjustment' and 'new beginnings'. Is he hanging on to give us time to accept?

The Room has seen it all before. Those that come don't always depart through the door they entered. How many other families have suspended their lives within its walls? One day, all but one of us will walk out without glancing back and its shell will become the stage for another family's journey.

But, for now, the sun, moon and stars revolve around The Room.

Vanished
Laura Jan Shore

On the lawn this morning, a lump
of faded feathers. A parrot
nudges his limp mate.

All day, he waits
for those green wings
to flex and follow.

A bruise blooms
on my breastbone.
Everywhere couples:

heads angled
towards each other,
hands finding other hands.

I touch your talc grey ashes
to my tongue. Grit fails
to still the tumbling in my chest.

Curled on my side of the bed,
I picture your iris—
opalescent, beckoning.

I was baptised in your gaze,
the beam
of your affection.

When your lids closed,
the woman you saw
vanished.

Sunflowers

Ingrid Birgden

I didn't know how to stop his crying. The cashier in the hardware store called from behind the counter,

'What's wrong?'

He had got his fingers jammed in the car door. Stepping out, she squatted down and handed him a brightly decorated packet.

'I've got something for you. They'll turn into these,' she said, showing him the picture. My son's sobs subsided into gulps.

'True?'

'True.'

We planted the seeds along the Colorbond fence and watered them every other morning. He followed me with his watering can through the scatter of magpie calls. The fine spray tipped in a fan across the soil. When the sunflowers grew tall and vibrant, they transformed our garden.

When did our lives begin to unravel? Our son, bellowing with a voice that was breaking and his face pressed hard against the window. With cajoling then threats, his father and I pushed him onto the Minibus.

'Everyone has to go to school!' I cried.

A solitary figure in the back of the van, moving further from us, away from our care. The first student on, the last one off. Sometimes in the late afternoon, I rang the Special Unit, concerned by the delay.

'They had to chase him around the oval to get him onto the bus!' the voice on the other end chuckled.

And so here we are now, in this dark and opulent room, making a statement to the Royal Commission. I have no peace. The nightmares, the writhing, the palms pressed into eye sockets, the howls, the crawling horror that haunts us . . . it was the bus driver with his collaborators and an institution that turned its back on all of us. Over and over, in my dreams, I hurl open the heavy sliding door, I haul my son out of the bus and scream, 'Run home!' I drag all the boys out, they are all there, they keep spilling out, I shove them away, yelling, 'Go! Go!'

And after the staccato of pain, the terrible stillness of loss. If we could embrace him, ask for forgiveness, reassure him, promise to protect him from harm forever. But he died. He died of stomach cancer as though the acid of silence gorged on his trauma. Death can be so banal. It is a van slammed shut, drifting to the corner, turning, then gone. It is absence, dead leaves blowing across the street.

The house is dark. Before the end of the season, I shall brighten it with sunflowers. The promise of sunflowers once stopped my boy crying. I press my forehead against the window. We used to watch movies together here on the lounge, our shoulders leaning together companionably. I hope my body's memory never loses the imprint of that precious, precious touch.

Life Lessons
Rosalind Moran

A hesitant child, I never touched
The shaved heads of my male classmates
My friends were girls, and I? Too shy
To pat their bristle smooth skulls, laughing

Hair grows out and so does youth's shadow
It falls behind me in a dying light
I cut my hair to look professional
Combing a parting between pretty and respected

Unexpected; a guest uninvited, yet a spectre
We knew would one day dissect her; pluck her
Bare. Her hair now lining the nest
Of a carrion bird who turns food to cardboard.

I wish I had never had reason to touch
A bare head; tracing its ridges. My fingers
Placed on my mother's breast—and guided
So they might learn what it is we must watch for.

I am a Little Eye Breaking
Shari Kocher

The eye in the pebble spills its secret.
Ask Fellini. *Every pebble has its purpose,
even the stars.* I am the knot in the Not-I in motion.
I am a little eye breaking.

The ginger cat sleeps with one eye open
on the second folded bed under the peeling wallpaper.
How he got there between the locked door
and the sun going down on wherever he goes

in the daytime—I like to think my purpose
is to walk through walls like Peanut, but who
is it who wakes heavy with headache / uneven
the fake fur-ball / high-low / what-a-night / peanut-

crunching crowd. Such knots are hard to loosen.
Some keep count, but that was a long time ago.
Others carry stones in their pockets. Not-I.
Mine is an ovoid andesite found on a black-sand

beach that seeps sweet water from a spring-licked
cliff-face. The Not-I knows this place from the way
her feet light up like two souls walking the umber
side of shadow. What do feet remember?

Only the letting go when Joy shoots up like a geyser
knocking her sideways on hands and knees,
a pitted, perfect stone. Not-I, the hand
that cradles the sun packed with purpose,

wearing the sweetest of holes in my pocket.
Ah yes. All the odds uneven. The knots in the
I in motion beautifully jagged, purposefully
broken. *Even the stars.*

Brain Cancer
Ellen Shelley

The ocean lookout is an old friend
with its sheer cliff face
an expression for every occasion,

standing on magnitude, respectful of weight
hard knocks have made it steadfast
air carved by edge.

Peering over I lose myself.
Those recent conversations, shift of the sea,
try & forget people gone, as I am left returning . . .

Your body, a project . . .

Besieged & burnt,
& those dissected numbers, relentlessly climbed.

The loyalty of suspension,
remission a held breath.

So much ownership & no possession,
            having brings no sense of grasp . . .

Vines hang over the fence like loose skin.
Inside, lamps hover in each corner
spilling their yellow light on sallow skin.

But you aren't here.
Your vacated frame sits by a window,
air blows through
without lifting a thought.

Your blood, a memory.

Survival is where the steady drips flow,
logic starves in the chambers above,
where repairs are temporary & the floor still leaks.

Comfort is in the hands that remind
            how worthwhile the shake,

a mind floating in limbo
that place it all began.

Foreboding
Kim Waters

After stealing an apricot from the crate
in the garage,
you jumped into the puff-sleeved pool

in which I sat in two feet of water.

I watched you bite through the freckled skin,

then spit the knuckled stone
in a long afternoon arc over your head.

I can't remember your six year-old face,
but I can hear your laughter
pinwheeling the sky and I recall the way

you whirlpooled the next moment,

looking for more mischief to circle the day.

In a pamphlet I read that apricot kernels
contain a lethal form of cyanide poisoning.

It is another form of poison
that you have ingested,

and now, forty years later, your laughter

lays silent in a closed crate

as the words of a psalm
float in two feet of water
across the page of my hymn book.

You Don't Die When You Want To
Val Gadd

How many times have you heard people say, 'I'd be better off dead' or 'I wish I was dead?' I am writing this story to tell you, you just can't die because you are fed up with the world, or things aren't going your way, because there's always something to keep you here.

It is hard to imagine the incredulous state of disbelief you feel, when someone, a husband, a father a brother, dies suddenly, unexpectedly and so young. Nothing penetrates the fog your brain is in, not your children crying, not your son trying CPR, not your brother in law trying to hold onto him. Nothing registers. All you feel is a numbness that you will never see this vibrant human being ever again. How do you compute this? The colour of his skin is etched in your brain, as he lays slumped on the floor.

The morning arrives, you've had no sleep. That unreal feeling that something is missing in your life. You know you must get back to Brisbane, you know you must tell your fifteen-year-old daughter her father is dead. Some things you can't do on the phone.

Family arrives to take control, to try and organize us, to get us in the car, to drive us to Brisbane, my two sons and I, all dazed. Our daughter rushes excitedly out to meet the car. She's been expecting her Dad to come so she's changed from the usual jeans to a formal dress, hair done, high heels and make-up to surprise him. Next minute she's fainted and is on the ground, all her finery dirty and dusty. You seem to be seeing, but not seeing it.

You know it's all true, he's gone forever. How can you grieve when your children need you? How can you die when your mortgage broker is hammering you for house payments? How can you find words to comfort your family when all you want to do is disappear from this earth? No one can help because you are numb. You don't want help, you want to be on your own, curled up in a corner waiting for the pain to go away. The pain never goes away. Twenty-four seven you are in pain, but all around your life is moving on. How can it?

Eventually it's time to have to take charge of your life again, you are needed. You need a lifetime to grieve, not three months. You need to get back in the workforce, your kids need a home and a mother. They are not coping, so you put your grief on hold to give them what they need. Relations, friends are all there for you, but you are on the outside looking in.

Life does move on and you have no choice but to move with it. The grief, however, will always be lodged deep in your brain and your heart. Obviously, God, doesn't want you yet.

The Hoarders
Linda Harding

The ward is huge, bustling with nurses, doctors and far too many patients. It is loud and public. It is no place to die on a beautiful April day. The staff is efficient and kind. We are numb.

We go to your bedside and find you, as we have each day in this last week: pallid, clammy, sunken eyed, with that terrible greyness of approaching death, struggling to breathe, barely with us at times. We massage cream into your hands, ask you questions you don't have the energy to answer, tell you of things we are doing at home.

We report that we have cleaned out the garage. You moan. As a life long hoarder you are appalled. You are certain we have thrown out untold treasure. Did we not realize we might have needed it one day? We can't confess that we had to do something, anything, rather than stand here watching you die in this hospital bed.

'They talk about dying,' you wheeze, 'but they don't tell you . . . it's such . . . hard . . . work. I'm so tired'.

'Close your eyes Dad,' I murmur.

'No! No stay with me, stay awake!' It's Mum. Reality is sinking in; all the years together are about to end. The future is vanishing, like the treasure in the garage.

'Is it ok if I bring the kids in to see you?' I ask. The grandsons, 7, 4 and 2 are waiting with their father in the garden.

You gasp out 'Yes'

I go out to get them, and when they arrive, you have transformed.

Superhuman, you sit up straight, back upright against the pillows. You greet them softly; ask them how they are and what they have been playing. You listen to them, answer their questions, kiss each one tenderly and tell them you love them, watch and wave as their father takes them outside once more.

Then you slump, utterly spent, grey and dying again. Where did the strength come from for that last goodbye Dad? Where had you stored that? Determined their last glimpse of you would be their gentle, loving Pa, you became the person they knew, one last time.

The nurse pulls the curtains around your bed, enclosing us in a blue cotton womb. The bustle and noise continue around us while the final act plays out.

It's distressing to see your struggle and pain. The doctor tells me he is amazed you're still here. Within the hour we watch you leave the grey shell of your body. Your heart stops beating, your magnificent heart that loved so well, and with that final beat, you leave us your legacy.

We hoard now, Dad. We hoard you. We stockpile each memory of your 63 years of life and love; we tuck them away to be brought out 'one day'. They are our treasure. We need every single one. I needed this one today.

I needed to remember how a grandfather's love conquered death for a final goodbye.

Galloway
Haibun / Tanka
The Poet Mj

The neigh is gone, the whinny and nickers, are deep. Hold the stars, the lost black hole is horse heaven. Hoof shaped, mane flairs, rump contours, those clouds gallop my vision of your figure, drifts. Mood canter in rage tides. Symbols clang, gong vibrates in ribs prison. Prisons of hallucination. I am bare foot on gravel, coral seaweed graves. Stomping goes past in rubber circles, whine metal tin. Smelt leather soap with honey wax, dust scattered lines. Beam of flowing crimpled tail gone in the hidden myth-mist of landscapes. Bellow rumpled rumble, belly of hunger, lost rides in the sand. If we could swim one with the ocean coastline like the film, I think I am growing hooves, lengthening face, mane hair strikes my blaze. Time is stardust in this black hole galaxy.

flying change brooding
      circumnavigate hooves, stir
           whimsical shying
                commission collect trot, vice
                hot-blooded grief, entropy

The Problem of You
Aimee Sargent

You've been dead six months. I've visited you every week. I sit in front of your plaque in the graveyard and stare at your name for a while. We never talk. Just stare. A staring competition of sorts, though nobody ever wins.

'Alex?'

My Mum stands across the table from me as I eat my breakfast. Neil is beside her. You don't know Neil. He came on the scene about three months ago. A dating website. Mum likes him. What would you make of him?

'Alex, we need to talk to you.'

They sit.

I reach for my drink. The glass is wet and my hand slips.

'Neil and I have decided to move in together.'

It is here that I understand the problem of you dying. It was not your actual death but your aftermath.

I drop my spoonful of sodden cereal and lean back.

'We've decided to sell the house. We'll live at Neil's place. I know it's a lot to take in but this is going to be good for us.'

I grab my glass, stand and skull its contents. Then I take my dishes to the kitchen sink.

'Alex, what was that?'

'Apple juice.'

'It was fizzy.'

'So?'

She looks at the kitchen bench where a half full bottle of cider waits.

'It's nine o'clock.'

'So?'

'Alex, please sit down. I want to talk with you.'

'We've done that.'

'Alex, we've got an offer on the house already. We need to make a decision in the next few days.'

'By all means, go ahead. You put the house on the market without telling me, so do whatever the hell you want.'

I run up the stairs to my room. I pace its length, looking around for something. I don't know what. I feel a rising pressure inside me. I pick a permanent marker up off my desk, enter your room and shut the door. It is neat and tidy once more. Your scent has been lost. I grab your bottle of Lynx and spray it. I stand on your bed and write on the wall in big, black, permanent letters: I HATE YOU. I write it over and over down the wall and then write more.

I HATE YOU
I HATE YOU
I hate you
I hate you
i hate you
i hate u
This is you: . . .
All people ever seem to say these days is sorry
When in doubt, move a pawn. That's what you used to say.
What if you've got none left?

'I remember when I was young and the
world had just begun and I was . . . '
Just was. That's enough sometimes.
1988-2013
It just occurred to me it's kind of ironic you died in Spring
Lots of people die in Spring
Lots of people die all the time
Does that make your death insignificant?

Lyric taken from 'I Remember When I was Young' by Matt Taylor. 1973. Album: *Straight as a Die*.

I'm losing my patients
Hilton Koppe

The blank death certificate sits in front of me, housed in its bland beige pad. No matter where a life starts, where it journeys, the Medical Certificate of Cause of Death is the concluding punctuation mark on a person's medical narrative.

I approach the completion of the death certificate with reverence. My final task in the care of a patient. A moment to pause. Reflect. Say goodbye. To honor their life within the rigid confines of a bureaucratic document.

This ritual is becoming increasingly frequent.

As a GP in a rural area for thirty years, my patients have grown older with me. Despite medicine's advances and my best efforts, they are dying. It is their time. As my wise grandmother taught me before she died, *'Mein lieber Gott vergisst niemanden.* My dear, God forgets no one.'

I'm losing my patients.

Just last month, I lost three.

Lilly was an elegant matriarch. She was my oldest patient. Each of her frequent visits to me ended with her gently touching my arm and saying 'Bless you Hilton'. I had cared for her husband Don before his death. Now it was Lilly's turn. Her heart was failing. 'I hope that one night I will go to sleep and wake up dead. Just like Don did'. Her wish came true a few weeks ago. Who is going to bless me now?

Len had been a child during the bombings of London during the war. I had once ruined his Christmas by advising that he go to hospital to have a heart pacemaker inserted. He would have died without it. He wasn't ready for that. The pacemaker kept him going for another decade. Not always easy years. But 'better than the alternative'. Len was a poet. Each visit to me was accompanied by the gift of a poem, 'from when the muse was upon me'. The last time I saw him he told that he was feeling better than he had for years. Another gift. He woke up dead a few days later.

Reg's children and grandchildren were patients of mine. When Reg moved to our town with his wife, they became my patients too. Reg was a lovable rogue with a wicked sense of humor. He was fiercely independent. Unflinchingly loyal to his wife, who had advancing dementia, shielding her from 'interfering do-gooders'. Reg dropped dead at home without warning. Out of sight beside his bed. It took two days for his family to discover what had happened, as in his wife's mind, he was just out doing the shopping. The police called me when his body was discovered. I am haunted by the memory of seeing him lying face down on the floor, so very very very dead.

I finish writing the death certificate. I walk out to greet my next patient. The waiting room is full. Many familiar faces look my way. I am troubled by a nagging thought. A persistent pestering question: 'I wonder who'll be next?'

Blackie
Annette Mullumby

that day I forgot
to shut the gate
I ran all streets calling you

a neighbour came
with a bloodied bundle

her loud tears
shrank my sorrow

I could not mourn
your stiff tailed greeting
warm muzzle in my hand
rough scarred hide

our cupped bodies
in the hollow
of the old mattress

Pomegranate
Ella Jeffery

It's winter and she has grown
so thin. She is cutting a pomegranate,
which her dissolved lover bought
and left in her apartment
along with a few other things—reading
glasses, a library book that sits
above the television accruing fees, radiant
with dust. As she cuts she tells me
that today her tape measure
recoiled and sliced the flesh
of her palm while she measured
a client's kitchen for an island bench.
I darken our glasses with more wine
and imagine each yellow inch
rattling across a stranger's
floorboards, the nick of shock
in her throat before she stood again
and asked for a towel. She says he gave
her a few tissues and an address
to which she could email the quote.
The pomegranate rolls on either side
of her knife, two halves
wobbling like dollars about to fall,
and inside them hardness
and clots of colour that redden
the bandage on her palm.
What can I do but stay
for a week, sit beside her
while she eats? She is almost through
the dark half of this year.

Abandoned Theatre
Carolyn Abbs

Holocaust Memorial, Amsterdam

each visitor   falls silent   as they enter
this once luxury theatre   now

a hollow   without a roof

the air   hangs   chokingly thick
in remembrance—

cold granite plaques reach skywards
engraved with lists and lists   of names—

innocent people   assembled here
their dark shapes   huddled together—

I want to leave, but a volunteer insists
I go up the modern stairs to the museum

sepia photos span walls like a terrible merry-go-
round   a nightmare   rattle of trains

and then in a glass case, small as a crib   a child's
worn grey clothes   pinned flat   as a dead moth—

The Spare Room
Harrison Saich

Mum keeps my brother's ashes in a box in the spare room.

Our spare room used to be full of Dad's stuff because he slept in there most nights. When he left, he took all of that stuff. Now there's a lot of space in the spare room, but I don't know where Dad sleeps anymore.

My best friend, Adam, has a spare room too. His is full of Lego, books and a dusty bed. And me. Tonight, I'll be sleeping in the dusty bed in Adam's spare room.

'Dinner is ready,' says Adam's Dad.

'Coming!' says Adam's sister. Adam's sister, Georgia, has red cheeks and is comedy gold, but Adam doesn't seem to think she's funny at all. I mean, he laughs when she's around, but I don't think he's laughing *with* her.

'That's not fair,' says Adam, 'Why doesn't Georgia have to eat as much as I do?'

'Because you're two years older than her,' says Adam's mother, no-nonsense style.

'But that means she'll finish before me, which means she'll get dessert before me.'

Adam has a point.

'Blame capitalism, Adam,' says Adam's Dad.

'Yeah, Adam, blame capitalisation,' says Georgia.

She looks happy for a moment, but then Adam does the laugh that might not be a laugh *with*.

'It's *capitalism*, dingus,' he says, flicking a pea at her. Now Georgia looks sad and that makes my stomach feel rooky.

When I feel rooky at home, Mum lets me do the thing where I put the tips of my fingernails under the tips of her fingernails. She usually hates it but lets me anyway.

After dinner, Adam and I build a submarine-aeroplane-racing car out of Lego.

'Should I ask Georgia if she wants to play?' I ask.

'Nah,' says Adam, 'She's boring.'

Later, when it's Bed Time, I lay down in Adam's dusty spare room but I can't sleep. I haven't felt this rooky for a while, not since I realised that all old women look like old men, and all old men look like old trees.

I get out of bed.

YOU'RE NOT BORING, I write on a piece of paper; I slip it under Georgia's door.

Outside, the wet grass feels nice on my cracked feet and the asphalt is cool. My house is only two blocks from Adam's so I follow the moon home.

'Are you OK?' says Mum, opening the door to let me in.

I've never noticed it before, but our house smells like apricots.

'I'm OK, Mum,' I say, 'My stomach feels rooky. Can I sleep in your bed tonight?'

'Of course,' she says, 'I'll ring Adam's parents and let them know. Go hop in bed.'

Before I do, I go into the spare room and get the box of my brother's ashes off the shelf.

'Goodnight, darling,' says Mum.

I know she sees the box because her cuddle is so tight it hurts.

'Goodnight,' I say.

Mum keeps my brother's ashes in a box in the spare room.

Just not yet.

Effie (1900–1951)
Beth Spencer

In this suburban living room
my father and five siblings sit
around a table with a tiny grey
photograph of their younger
suited selves lined up
beside their mother's grave.
The air dances for a moment
and thickens.

Thirty years collapse.
An invisible thread grips.
No-one speaks, or moves
(because it is here in the room).
What is this thing that
cannot be killed, or caught?
Or locked up, or tamed,
or swallowed whole?

That can change the air
with its cry? (The pulse of it.)
Weight it with concrete
and ten guineas of flowers.
Still years later
it will find its way in.
Like that wall of water
loving the hairline crack.

What remains
Frank Russo

We long for signs at night, willing them to appear on the fresh coat of paint
like lines drawn across a rock-face, elemental as the horses of Lascaux.

We yearn for the ballpoint pen to upend itself—to skim across the table's surface
as if commanded; for the photograph securely hung, to drop from its hook,

to knock the vase of lillies from the estranged cousin off its perch.
The air thick with presence, the way the lines of a song fill the room

with more than just notes, how the oldest memory of the ocean
can stand the hairs on the night air's nape.

Outside, the sounds of nocturnal life: the hiss of rhino beetles on the porch,
their serrated horns like scythes to thresh the earth,

the scuttle of geckos across the flyscreen mesh, their high-pitch chk-chk-chk,
a kind of morse code through which the departed might communicate,

and from the scrub, the haunting calls of curlews—
how they mock us, imitating the cries of the half-returned.

You close the doors to this Kecak chant, and you're alone with the detritus of the day:
the rot of lettuce that lingers from the tray of sandwiches, the swirl of ants

around the wound of a discarded mango. You pass the new walk-in robe,
stuffed with clothes to be bagged, the CPAP machine to be given away,

and you're left with the consolation of half-remembered words, with the thought
that most matter can't be seen. You wonder if these things will be enough;

how when you took the album of photographs to the funeral home, the parents of the boy
who died on the river, were there to collect his ashes,

gently handed over like a box of medication,
too small and insubstantial to be theirs.

In the morning there's the stillness of the pool, shimmering like a talisman
that's attracted its night-time cull of bugs and leaves.

On the limestone deck, a lone stork is reflected on the water's surface.
It stands so still, at first you mistake it for a statue amongst the concrete planters.

You've never seen such a bird by this pool, and you question why
it would rest there, in this season, without its flock,

on this morning of all possible mornings,
and through the trees a sudden gust,

that resembles a dozen magpie geese rising.

The Telling
Steve Coates

The police car crossed the cattle grid and crept slowly along the driveway to the house. I could see Joan in the passenger's seat. They've come for the heater, I thought. It seemed like overkill to involve the law but I knew we were outsiders and I was beginning to learn the ways of these tiny towns. Kids at the bus stop boasted that the local cop's loyalties went cheap, that the publican gave him free cases of beer in exchange for turning a blind eye.

I don't remember the cop's name; Daryl springs to mind, but that might just be because 1980s Australia seemed to have an oversupply of moustachioed Daryls. He and Joan both looked serious, but they didn't mention the heater. Where was my mother?

I said she and my sister were on their way back from Sydney with the last load of our stuff. We'd moved to the area six weeks before in an abrupt lifestyle change, after dad was offered a job working for Joan's husband. At the time my parents were in the rosy glow of a new adult friendship with them, of the type where kerosene heaters were freely loaned; four weeks later they'd fallen out.

Joan seemed smaller than when I'd seen her last. She hung back as Maybe Daryl looked in me in the eye and, in the direct and formal language of a tv cop, told me there'd been an accident earlier that day and he was sorry to say my father had been killed.

Just like that.

They took me to Joan and Norm's house in the village and left me alone in the tiny lounge room. Should I scream, break something, make some dramatic gesture? Even cry?

The tv was showing an old western. Bang! Bang! Another two Indians down. I'd never realised that death was everywhere, so unremarkable.

It might have been 15 minutes or three hours but eventually I was back at the farm, awaiting the arrival of mum and Sue. Joan and Maybe Daryl lurked respectfully in the shadowy lounge room behind me so I could destroy my family with the news myself; I might only be 14 but I was the man of the family now!

Mum's face.

That night the tears came, some kind of madness sneaking in behind them. As we ventured deeper into this unknown new world its surprising non-boundaries were revealed: mum could threw a cup of tea across the room and leave it seeping quietly into the carpet, I could take cigarettes from her pack and smoke them with her, my sister could change from happy-go-lucky to anxious and timid for ever. And we could tell ourselves wild grasping crazinesses: they didn't know him and how he was indestructible; they'd made a mistake and identified the wrong person; he'd ring up any minute and we'd laugh how we'd laugh.

Today We Should Have
Elanna Herbert

been at that warung in a Kuta laneway
eating *Gado-gado*. the one we went to

last time when you told the kids Ratus
ratus crawling along the rafters was

an Indonesian marsupial and my
teenage daughter ordered Shepherd's Pie

because for once she missed her mother's
cooking. instead we buried our father

in the grave of our mother. we threw
disjointed flowers from my garden onto

exposed soil. bruised colour holding down her
bones. then two daughters, a granddaughter

the tall cousin from Sydney and the only grandson
carried our father's coffin to this place overlooking

the ocean. we stood together. we watched.
his coffin lowered into earth. that moment

rolled in breaking with emotion and we threw
the last flowers on top. later at the club we

both ordered pepper steak, a white wine. he knew
the routine. we sat. we watched. the ocean.

Don't Let it Bring You Down*
Shaun Maguire

At the Fingal lookout
the steel railing frames a view
of the blues of sea and sky.
In the distance
a plume offered to the air
signals a whale's presence
on its migration to the birthing waters
in the north.
Scratched tourist names
mark the length of railing—
as they scuttle towards eternity.

From the darkness
a soft wind plumes
through the framed window.
It touches the skin
offering a promise
before leaving without sign.
It was a purity born of the air
a moment lived completely,
unchangeable
and then it was gone.

Where the birds no longer whistle
'and a blue moon sinks from the weight of the load'#
a grave is marked by a final scratch,
and yet
something remains in the air,
Unchangeable.

* Title of song released by Neil Young, 1970
# a line from the song 'Don't Let It Bring You Down'

Dreams
Hessom Razavi

He visits
at the doorway or
breakfast table, natural as life,
smile made from sunrise and
Persian cedars, coursing me like a
hundred *Bandari* hands, like thrills
from *bulbuls* and divans,
bleating to crescendo in
tears from a sixteen-year-old spring
that remembers
Baba.

We hug,
hard enough to bruise,
as if bodies could merge to
crush lost time, forge new dents,
handprints to outlast the waking,
pull him back by force or
imprint his smell 'til he
visits again, darling *Baba*
in the apricot light
of dreams.

I wake
from his cedar tree,
arms like boughs, warmth of
my safest nook—*Baba*—
to clutch and grab
at nothing, will myself back,
stung by reality
and shaking into the crook
of my own arm.

Bandari: music and dance from South Iran, distinguished by the fluttering of hands.
bulbul: singing thrush nightingale; a recurring motif in Persian poetry.

Too Much For Words
Fiona Murphy

We sit up against the headboard, the quilt tented by our bent knees. I've started going through my art history books that have gone touched since last winter. Even though there aren't any more hospital visits to rush to or paperwork to fill out, reading still feels like a luxury. I can't imagine painting again.

The bed creaks as Phil rests his novel on his lap and grabs his dictionary off the bedside. He flicks through it, ready to pull out another word. He acts as if he can no longer assume anything; everything has to be validated, precise and clear.

I keep still, forcing silence into the bedroom. I try to study the painting that lies in front of me. It is a nude. The model has been arranged to maximise the pleasure of the viewer, yet the composition is so dull it's difficult to pretend that I'm completely engaged in the awkward mess of limbs. Phil continues to flick through his dictionary, hunting for a word. My jaw tightens. We haven't spoken since the funeral. It's easy to pretend that everything is ok during the daylight, as I can always rearrange the pantry or weed the garden. I dread when the sun goes down, the wait until morning feels like an eternity.

Hours later, a thought rises up from my familiar rubble of ruminations. I pull back the covers, pick up the book and look at the nude in the bathroom. Her skin is so even it almost melts into the backdrop of careless drapery. An evanescent being slowly evaporating. I feel decisively sick. Time slides on, soon we will all disappear. I wonder if I still want to keep trying.

A month later the lightbulb bursts in our bedroom, its hot fizz showers down. We sit in the dark, shocked. The shards of glass sprinkle the sheets. Slowly we slide out of the bed and pad across the floor. I fossick through the kitchen drawer for a torch. My skin feels scratchy. I turn around and see Phil stretched out on the couch. His arm draped over his eyes. A rage runs through me.

'You could help, you know.'

'What?' His voice is muffled by his arm.

'Instead of just lying there, you could get up and help me.'

Phil turns his head and studies me in the dark. 'It'll be easier to fix the mess in the morning. I'll sleep here, and you can grab the bed in the spare room.'

My breath sits high and tight in my chest. I grip the torch, feeling its brutish heft. '*The spare room*?' I swing the torch towards him.

Phil ducks out of the way.

'Phil, it has only been ten months. It hasn't even been a year.'

'I'm sorry Sylvia, I didn't mean to say it,' he stands up and reaches towards me. I start to sink, weak kneed and exhausted. The effort to argue is too much for words.

In Tumult
Kathryn Fry

> In memory of Denise Frost, 1947-2015
> after Philip Wolfhagen's 'Surface Tension #3'

His canvas beside her. *How the textures leap
close*, she said. I think of a water strider's long
legs spread out above the surface, but this

is no pond's tension, nor is it the force and fury
of white-water, drowning cries. They wrap around
you, his waxed blues, and lock like the darkest

hours of racing thought, the lurch and roll and curl.
When we spoke, even her eyes listened then. I see
them still and wonder have I loved enough.

He loved to brush rhythms (the drama of *Gloriana*)
on linen, his strip of sea without bird or boat and
fading to the palest sky. She knew art, I knew

briefly the light she cast. But the sudden
shocking loss of her, so young still, churned
like an ocean in tumult, the tears in his sea. Yet,

after the cathedral of grief, spoken and sung,
this then, her parting gift: that we would leave
with the strain and swirl of *Here Comes the Sun*.

The Window
Narelle Absolom

I lost him when I was just starting. Grown, but young and learning about life. He was older—but not much wiser—and thoughtful and kind. All of life's possibilities were ahead of us. He promised he'd never hurt me.

'I'm your brother,' he said, as he poured a spoonful of water into my eye to unstick my new contact lens. Even in that ridiculous moment, he knew how to make me feel safe. A protector, always.

Despite his promises, he left one day. Off to sleep, with no one watching. A soft breath, then gone.

Things were never the same after. He did what he always promised not to. The hurt was a punch to the gut that kept on punching. Twenty years and still I double over, winded and full of shock.

I dream of a window. Something magical but true. The window shows me what life would be like if he were still here. In the window, everything is the same—except he is alive.

I look back at moments from my real life and see him. The window lets me have a glimpse, a taste of what might have been. Him standing up at my wedding, grinning with pride; laughing and gasping over holiday snaps from trips to Japan and Greece and New Zealand; a visit to the hospital when I'm groggy from the pethidine, post-appendectomy; the time I was brave enough to put on Christmas dinner all by myself. All the joys and sorrows—big and small—that would have been different if he'd been there.

It was dangerous, this window. Sweet and bitter at the same time; alluring and addicting. I return to it again and again, tasting the past that never was.

It is a difficult thing indeed, to pull myself away and come back to the everyday routine life of the real world each time. To my husband, to my friends, to my job and pastimes.

I close the curtains on the window. Time doesn't heal all wounds. It just makes it easier to not break down all the time. But the pain remains. The grief. The loss.

One day, I fear—or maybe hope—I'll be stuck in the window forever.

But what then? I too would become someone else's window dream. A ghost of what might have been.

Perhaps that is all life is. A collection of memories shuffled and sorted, to be visited and wondered on, like tomes on a dusty bookshelf. A bright spark in a melancholy night.

I pull back the curtain and peek. He is waiting. He smiles with eyes that will never open again. Just one look. One more can't hurt.

I lean in.

And fall.

The Secret Life of Mum
Cindy Bennett

When Dad died, it was almost a relief. He had been in pain for years and it was only his determination not to leave Mum that kept him going. But she did the one thing he couldn't forgive.

She put him in a home and six days later he surrendered to death. His struggle was over.

Mum was guilt ridden. She could no longer care for him at home but still she was determined to feel bad, which had always been her way.

In the following months she started to get out by herself and began to, begrudgingly, enjoy being her own person. She was a little confused at the lack of sympathy she received as a new widow even though, living in a retirement village, nearly everyone was a widow; she was still a little put out. Perhaps if he had died when she was younger, she mused, she may have been elevated to the widow status she felt entitled to.

She confided things didn't feel right; something was wrong and we talked about the sudden impact of being alone after a lifetime of having at least one other person around but she didn't think that was it.

She had her heart checked as her family had a habit of dropping dead from heart attacks and she was relieved to get a clean bill of health.

The next day we found her dead in her chair.

Her death was like a stab in the heart; perhaps because it was unexpected, perhaps because we weren't close or perhaps because it robbed her of living a life free from obligation and duty for the first time. It just wasn't fair.

Being the writer of eulogies in the family, the task fell to me to honour Mum in the same way I had honoured Dad. But the words just wouldn't come. Mum's life had no funny stories, no amusing anecdotes. Mum had spent her life in an almost permanent cloud of doom, shaming herself for past regrets, complaining of the drudgery of being a wife and a mother and always expecting the worst—and here we were.

So imagine my surprise to hear stories of what a fun person she was. How thoughtful and kind she was and what wise counsel she gave. This was a woman I did not know. Why had she not shown this side to us? Why did my Mother feel the need to live her joy in secret? Would sharing it with her children have contaminated it? Lessened it? Did she hate her life as a wife and mother so much?

I grieve for my Mother, for the life she had but derived no joy from. I grieve for the side of her she hid from us, the fun, kind, thoughtful woman. I am heartbroken she felt the need to live her joy in secret. But mostly I grieve because she taught me to do the same. Time to change.

Sadness is a Long Tunnel
Rose Lucas

an underground space not made
to accommodate the size and heft and panic
of a person
        struggling and
exhausted in the dark;

sometimes I think about the impossible simplicity of
grass and sunlight,
a world in which the torn is sutured,
where there is only
the faintest line of scar down the length of your chest
to remember the sharpness of this
edge—
        the body's memento—

but then I am returned to encroaching closeness
the inevitability of here:
the dankness of its thinning air,
the stumble of unseen tree roots and
scuttlings in the shadows;

disoriented,
there is only the hope of rising
        not deepening, of
                sometime
meeting the earth at
the softness of its gentling lip.

Ready to go
Alex Grantham

On the ward, dim lights signalled the nurse's station. A nurse approached and Margaret bristled.

'Has Charlie McGrath been moved?' She asked the nurse.

'He's in there. Take your time.' She patted Margaret's arm. 'I'm sorry for your loss.'

'What have I lost? I haven't lost anything. He's still with me.' Margaret pointed to her chest. 'In here.' She paused at her unexpected outburst.

'Do you need something to collect his things in?' The nurse asked. Margaret nodded as she looked above the nurse's head into the distance.

'Of course.' The nurse opened the door to Charlie's room and handed her a plastic bag. Margaret stepped into the chilled room and closed the door behind her. Like yesterday, her pale husband rested on the bed but today his chest didn't move. A heaviness leaked into her muscles. They'd lied to her. He was meant to come home. He was meant to have more time. She reached into the drawer next to the bed and took his wallet, a toothbrush and a photo of their family. His wedding ring caught her eye under the hospital lights. Margaret placed his cold hand on her face. *You used to say only the good die young. You made me laugh so much I forgot we were getting older.* She took his things and put them in the bag. She kissed his cool forehead that would never be warmed by her touch again. The door flew open and two men rushed into the room.

'What are you doing here?' Margaret's severe tone shocked them. She grasped Charlie's hand harder.

'We've come to take him.' Two orderlies stood in the doorway.

A stress rash spread across Margaret's chest like a strangling weed.

'We're busy. Come back later.'

They turned and left. *Jeepers, Charlie, what's the emergency? You've already died.* Margaret smiled at the irony but Charlie didn't smile back. He didn't gawk at the audacity. His eyes didn't flicker. He had left. She checked just to make sure that there was no breath from his lips. She was ready to go. She put his hand by his side and opened the door. The orderlies stood outside the room.

'You can take him now.' She whispered. 'He's ready to go.'

When Are We Women
Kathryn Lyster

here we are in the back of a bakkie
cruising up sanipass sleet drops

to lesotho mountains her
head's shaved ringworm

from their white cat charlie
in durban matching green

fullofholeshandknittedjerseys
no shoes blue

lips snotty colds when gun
died we slept in bedroom under

mountain banshee
wind howling fairy ring

fullmoon shell feathers dried
flowers beachstones at breakfast

rosa told us she woke
after midnight looked over i

was lying in withered
arms of our passed

away grandmother we ate
pawpawpaw feinbos

honey swim in bracken
water river flows

to sea brown kelp black
penguins one bloated

dead in dunes from sand-
storm we floated

her backout to sea we
are seven eight running

through sugarcane fields wild
coast air molasses sky burning.

Want

Jemma van Loenen

When I was a little girl I wanted to be a mum. Well, it was a thing you said wasn't it? Pre-conditioned, social expectation, innate maternal drive, survival of the species—whatever it was, it was something I thought, something I expected, something I wanted.

Now—well, now it is not so much a thing of want. Want doesn't even factor into it really. As a child you think it is simple—everybody makes babies, that's what you do when you grow up. When you grow up you realize, like most things, nothing is simple. Yet people still ask—'Do you want kids?'—as if it is a thing of want.

I tried, it's not like I didn't try. I mean at least I had a partner, not everyone has a partner to try with. Ten, eleven, twelve years . . . At some point you have to accept your lot. You are probably not going to be a mum. Want is irrelevant. Want won't get you a baby. So I let go.

Of course as fate would have things suddenly you find out you are going to be a mum. Life loves irony. It loves to turn everything upside down just when you think you understand it. So things change, we prepare, we plan, we rejig our ideas of ourselves and of—well—our family.

But herein ends the title of mum. One in four pregnancies end in miscarriage. Two in four if you're aged over forty. The odds are not great really. Life holds on by a tendril. But the tease does not end there as I fall pregnant again—I'm a mum again, for a bit. As I said it's a fifty percent chance of loss when you're over forty.

Want. I want—yes—but you don't get everything you want do you? Didn't your mum teach you that? I want ice cream. I want new shoes. I want to watch TV. I want to go to Paris. I want to party. I want to sleep. I want a baby. You don't always get what you want.

What I want is not the question. What I want is not actually even a thing that life or fate or whatever it is that oversees the balance of the universe, might consider. I have no control. It is not mine to control. Nor is it mine to behold, like my babies. Life and death make their own way. Yet, I still want.

Want will not hold me. Want will not fill me. Want only makes the ache worse. But I go on wanting. I cannot not want. If want is to desire it is also to lack and lack I do. When people ask if I want kids, perhaps they are really asking if I lack kids. Want? Yes. Lack? Yes. There is not much more I can do.

The Breathing Earth
Kimberley Zeneth

last days
the wizened ace of her
lies curled
absent from this world
the earth already beginning
to breathe through her

she stirs, balancing, drinks
rests to blink in the sunlight
senses still alive to turns of the breeze

being in the desert taught me
how small we each are, how vast

our shared living
a wide flow across eons

she has been my brief familiar
will circle me onwards

the breathing earth rises
falls softly under my hand
the thin voice rests
vague hum of her gratitude
tiny vibrations through finger bones

I sense an invisible rocking deep below
an eating up of things that must go
a body finished

black, tinged a reddish brown

the breathing earth
is ready for her

What Jane will Never Know
Heather Thomas

Jane stood looking down the length of the hospital bed at the old, dying man, her grandfather. 'Don't say anything. Don't say anything.' The mantra echoed in her head. At the same time she wanted to ask 'How could you? And did you, in the end, believe her?' But she said nothing, asked none of these questions.

Her grandfather lingered, living for a few more days. During that time Jane resisted her mother's pleas to visit him in the hospital again. She was afraid she'd not be able to hold her tongue for a second visit.

Now she would never know.

At the funeral Jane was reminded of simpler times when she had been a young child in the care of her loving grandfather. He'd take her out to the back yard to feed bluey, the pet blue tongue lizard, with tiny bits of chopped meat. Bluey was trapped in a kind of lizard park; a landscape of dirt, rocks, sticks and leaves contained in an old bath with some wire stretched over the top. When Bluey stopped taking meat, indicating he'd had enough, Jane's grandfather would let her use some of the tools in his workshop. Her favourites were the planes and hand drill.

At the funeral her uncle talked about her grandfather's war neuroses and how it wasn't really acknowledged when he came home in 1945. He was just expected to get on with life by getting to know the children who had been born while he was away and returning to work as a carpenter.

Jane felt herself choked with conflicting emotions, and smothered a sob with her handkerchief. She had loved her grandfather and felt sympathy for the young man he had been. But her mother's revelations of her own sexual abuse at the hands of his father had destroyed the stories she had believed about the family. Her mother had been 12 when she told her parents about the abuse which had been happening to her for years. Her mother's emerging sense of self had been beaten back by the disbelief of her parents. It would only re-emerge, malformed and fragile, years later, through painstaking therapy. But after the revelations the abuse had stopped. Feeling a warped sense of duty or, perhaps, a determined forgiveness, her mother had served her father as he aged; cooking, washing and cleaning for him as he became increasingly frail.

Could *she* forgive, Jane wondered, as she sat with the hard pew beneath her. Maybe, if she knew her grandfather had finally believed her mother. If there were any sign he had done something to protect his daughter. But the only person who could give her the answers she sought was laid out in the coffin before her. And now she would never know.

Visiting Mum

Zoë Disher

Today Mum's as chirpy as a baby budgie. She looks like one too, with her wobbly head and her skin covered in crazy wrinkles.

'Hello, Wendy,' she says as I pick my way through the half-asleep wheelchairs.

Wendy's my sister. She doesn't visit Mum anymore. There's no point, she says, it's too upsetting.

'Hello, Mum.' I kiss her gently.

Mum coos and pats my arm, 'You've lost weight, Wendy.'

I wheel her to her room where I can fuss over her; smooth her downy hair and tidy her things.

'Nurse,' she says to me, frowning, 'why don't my children visit? Are you keeping them out?' Her fingers claw at my sleeve.

Maybe Wendy's right. Maybe there is no point.

I pat her hand and stroke her hair. Sometimes that works better than anything else. I sing snatches of a lullaby I learnt from her, long ago.

'Hush, little baby,' we sing, mother and child.

I give her a ball of wool I've brought—as blue as the open sky. Occasionally objects trigger memories and bring Mum back to me, for a little while.

She fumbles with it as I water her pot plants.

And then she talks—to me.

'Sue, you must remember your brother.'

'Mmmm,' I murmur as I pick away the dead flowers. There is no brother, just Wendy and me.

'They took him away from me.'

I pause, a prickle in my stomach. I shouldn't go with her into this. She'll become agitated. I should change the topic.

So why do I ask, 'Who did?'?

'The doctors.' She shrinks into her chair and her eyes dart around the room. I don't know what to say. Her mind's wandering, isn't it?

'They told me to forget. They said, 'Never mind, dearie, go home and forget about it and try again.''

I look at her face, her eyes bright with memory. 'Is this true?' I say.

'I knew he was dead. He wasn't ready to be born, poor mite—only half grown.' Her fingers flutter and tangle the wool. 'They didn't even let me see him!'

'When . . .'

'How could I forget? Throw away the only scrap of life he'd got? I couldn't forget about my little boy.' She taps her heart, dangling the wool.

'He was always right here.'

My own heart has stopped, I am sure.

'But sometimes I get forgetful, now.' Mum whispers this—it's a secret. 'You remember for me, Sue. His name was Robert. You remember so I don't forget him.'

I hug her, craning over her chair to reach her. I cry with her. I cry for her and for me—and for Robert.

'I'll remember,' I say.

By the time I leave she is chirpy again. I wheel her back to the common room. 'Bye bye, Wendy,' she waves.

I smile back but I feel exhausted, bloated with this slow grief. And yet, I'm glad I came to see Mum today.

I'll call Wendy.

Earthing
Jane Frank

We cast no shadows
on chartreuse

Have only a watering can
a spade

A prayer about last trumpets
and a mortal body

Putting on immortality.
Coat what's left

In chrysanthemums and
coarse sand —

Ivory, lemon, Tyrian purple, red
and cover your smile

with turf and small talk. So
I crave extravagance —

Qin's army of terracotta warriors
to help you bide

Millennia without paint
or a tomb where

I can preserve you in words —
a new skin

Of all your letters that sustained me.
We turn to go

And I hear your patient voice
coaxing

The young gardenia
to grow

Departure
Natasha Parnian

We closed the door to the house
and returned the keys
and sat outside
as others came in
and painted its walls green
To mask the stains of our joys
that danced from the walls and
ripped apart the carpet
that had stains of Ararat cognac and remnants of my bridal bouquet
from circling to the raw joy of the Sazandar* that deafened our walls
These walls had been our only companion
collecting our thoughts
and sewing them into its embroidery
growing us warm
they became striped from the scent of our sweat
shaking from the shrieks of our sleeps
in those nights when we were kept up
from the hands of the teller of time
That controlled our fate
That dictated when we entered
And when we left
When we ate
and when we cried
When we fell in love
When we danced
and when we buried those we loved . . .
And when we took down their frames
packing up the prose they had brought from lands afar
We still stared at this house
as if it too,
would not disintegrate into soil
Like us.

*Traditional Armenian wedding band

At This End of Times
Elanna Herbert

i become obsessed with old photographs saving sorting sectioning
photo shopped images. rushing to complete this thing which was
always going to be too late. sifting handfuls of sepia ancestors.
scattered through your black and white childhood drops into place.
click-tight as a coin in a gumball machine delivering age-crisp

miniatures. country town South Australia during the war. no one
takes this care anymore my instagram kids will never understand how
long it took to shape an image that even mistakes are kept and
shadows in black and white grey tones still count. how a blurred
mistake—your father near the corrugated iron gate—speaks time

and place. a lifetime of wearing a hat, the swish of a hand. bits of a
lost thing i only remember in extracts. slanted, tipping from me and
all i have now are edges folded over untrustworthy memories. your
town in the 60s and 70s another skinny kid walking it dressed in
awkward adolescence. and here you are—wearing your South's

Football Club blazer—back before you found League found life.
moved away married had kids grew old. back when you couldn't
wait to see the next day—at twenty, or younger, thin, eager—then as
now to pick our family in team photos look for the skinny kid
standing like this. straight up one hand crossed over the other, holding

your wrist ready to take on the world. pants too loose shoes too
polished. standing on crushed gravel, your German mother's back
yard. fruit trees—aren't they always—and tins and pots and veggies.
i remember that yard—Old Man Saltbush crowding into town—a low
tide heat haze flooding the gulf and respite on the cool side of the

water tank. then a moment sharp as a newly found photograph. your
ancestor, 1872 glaring back at me. no one knew his image—this old
man wearing your forehead and that comb-over that embarrassed me
in 1974. i printed the photo. i wanted to touch it. to take it back to
you. to slip it in your pocket unseen by the shallow nurse, the short

doctor. slip it there for you to keep close—a road map at this end of
times—too soon you will know his face. so remember. once. now.
remember Dad. remember this is who you will walk there beside.

Dad
Emma Young

Dad becomes business valuations
A 30-year career equals four grand's worth of office equipment
Individually photographed, personality stripped
Printed on 17 pages with corresponding market values

Dad becomes a pharmacy
I'd say walking pharmacy but he'll never walk again
Levetiracetam (antiepileptic) kytril (antinausea) warfarin coversyl pramin dexamathasone haloperidol
fusemide buscopan nilstat metropolol mobic clozaepram amlodipine nexium

Dad becomes a series of tasks, a process
Wash his body, change his shit-bag, massage his wasted calves, once curved with muscle,
Cut his nails, brush his teeth, wash hair with a pre-soap-loaded cap
Shave and spray with Aramis, his favourite fragrance

Dad becomes ashes; 2kg, a surprising quantity that will need decanting
Given his instructions (home and the Kimberley)
So I and my soon-to-be fiancé traipse round Garden City
Looking for screw-lid containers that are Suitable

None are suitable. All are transparent. People usually like to see what is in their jars.
Aha! White porcelain, with—dammit—a clear window. It'll have to do. Jeez it's weird
You never imagine a future searching for ashes containers in kitchen shops
On the first day of Sunday trading in WA

Dad becomes countless photographs
An Eagles scarf, a funeral bookmark, emails, a black neck pillow that still smells like him
And a fear of losing even this; that holding the pillow will hasten the fading of the scent
What will I do with it then? Really I know the smell is just QV Wash.

What was that like, Dad? To know your daughter, who you had fed, clothed, bathed
Fed you, clothed you, bathed you, held a bottle over your shrivelled penis
I know you didn't want that to go on. None of us did, but still—
I would do that forever if that is what it took, Dad, to have you back

The Souls of Millions of Light Years Away*
Tristan Carey

If you stood outside
the universe looking back in
you would see

a steady fall of time —
not that of sand in glass
where grains gather space

and all yesterdays are
todays are
tomorrows are all

indistinguishable
words in a book
left out in the rain

signs to the souls of millions
of light years away —
from that vantage

all moments are found again
and looking long enough you would
witness the beginning and the end

when we first met
and when you left us
for the last time

*from Yayoi Kusama's *Infinity Mirrored Room
- The Souls of Millions of Light Years Away* (2013)

Uphill Triolets

i.m. N.B., after Natalie Diaz's 'Downhill Triolets'
Stuart Barnes

My grandmother hoovers up pills for nerves
(old-fashioned code for anxiety),
pours warmth into a tub with pastel-green curves.
Charcoal-haired, she echoes the quack: *For nerves.*
I splash in the water, strawberry preserves
astounding my mouth. *The buildin' society—
don't leave the house, darlin'!—shuts at four.* Nerves
lose themselves in a new brain: gold for anxiety.

My grandmother doesn't rise to fill the kettle.
Havin' a bad one her husband explains.
This winter his daphne lacks mettle,
miniature daffodils established in the kettle
outside have need of colour: trumpet, petal,
scape. This ivory-headed woman's brain's
whistling incessantly, like the kettle
inside. *Talk to her normal* her husband explains.

My grandmother was eulogised this morning.
The pastel-green bath's smooth water's cooling
while my father and his family are mourning.
Pink Moon's skipping at 'From The Morning':
'the endless summer nights' is a warning.
In my almond-shaped brain-bits, fast schooling.
My grandmother was eulogised this morning.
The pastel-green bath's edged water's cooling.

note: 'the endless summer nights' is from the Nick Drake song 'From The Morning'

Rearranging the paintings after they return from your Retrospective
Jane Frank

I can already hear nails
hammering in my head. Every

few seconds an empty wall
flashes by on a pre-sleep flat-

screen. Sometimes I see myself
taking a painting from the tall

pile on the living room floor
and placing it in a space where

it speaks the right way, and
in return, I say that it has rained

the whole of April—watch the
water pooling in the emerald

green field where the grass is
waving. I am counting the blades

now, the many strokes it took and
looking for evidence of where

the brush was loaded up, splayed
so the sky sieved it's heavy lilac

medley in a swathe of promise.
Home becomes a haven again

of interlocked polaroids: a life
shaken into sheets of alizarin

crimson, raw umber, ultramarine—
your name a contrasting colour

that jolts me, in a comforting way,
as I enter each new room.

Life After Death
Heather MacKenzie

It has been a year, a tumble of days. Life has continued somehow to explode around me every day. Roses have budded, flowered, faded in the sun. Sea rubbed pebbles on wet night beaches have glinted unseen in starlight, washed away again on tides. Seasons have turned and turned again. The river where the red rose floated with your ashes is the same but not the same. As I am the same but not the same.

I have returned to where we started

Sometimes I am ambushed by memories. Cunningly they come when least expected, reaching for a cup, hanging out washing, a line in a song, a word on a page. In the routine of days at times grief, then a surprising happy memory pops a champagne cork. I have given up feeling guilty about those. You would only laugh at me.

I have returned to where we started

There are times I want to share the words of some poem or book I am reading. Argue some point with you, blink a secret understanding across a crowded room, clink wine glasses. Write, write, write, talk, talk, talk to you. But I only have reminiscence re-runs. It's like binge-watching our relationship, the slips, the falls, the catches through the pass of years. I can remember the first time I saw your face and the last. The first word you said to me and the last. Between hello and goodbye nearly fifty years of grace notes.

I have returned to where we started

My Grandmother, searching for words
Seetha Nambiar Dodd

For Muthashi

She is searching for words set within a square grid in a book of puzzles. There is a list, next to the grid, of all the hidden words that need to be found. She circles each word as she finds it, ticks it off the list and smiles at me. 'Never give up,' she says. The words are all there, waiting to be found.

She is struggling to see the words as her eyesight worsens, so we get large-print puzzle books, and she continues searching. Despite this not being her first language, she does not give up until she finds the words. The words are all there, waiting to be found.

She is losing words. I know this is normal, because they warned me of her decline, but I am not prepared for the day I visit, and she has lost my name, and suddenly I am lost, floating in the confusion of her memory, drifting in the swirls of her mind. She is my base, my headquarters, my mothership. If she does not know who I am, who am I? Still, she doesn't give up. I remind her, she nods, she forgets. The words are there, and we find them together.

She is no longer searching for words, but this is not because she has given up. She is fighting, and the fight consumes all her strength. The words are still there, but we know she can't find them. Slowly, she slips away, and then the words are lost forever. Along with the words I wish I'd heard, and the words I wish I'd said.

Now it is up to us to search for the words. The soft, gentle words to inform family and friends of her passing. The correct, respectful words to write in her obituary. The weighty, healing words that fall from our hearts onto paper. The rich, evocative words to remember an entire life. We search for these words. There is no grid to contain the search. There is no list of all the hidden words that need to be found. There is no guide for grief. But we try. We don't give up. We find the words.

A Haibun For My Dying Mother
Rosemary Harper

On board the plane now
Sardines in cheap seats tight hot
Wish it were over.

Jetstar Flight JX234 to Brisbane can hardly be called luxury. It is a dreaded journey to more heat, traffic and a loved mother who sits, lies, passive and dreaming, her every physical need attended by strangers. Far from her daughter she sleeps, waiting, waiting, only for death.

The train leaves quickly
Electric, silent and fast
Rushing to the Home.

The journey to my Mother is relentless, I fight with my feelings all the way. To say I do not wish for this meeting is understatement. My whole being rails against this slow tortuous ending to a bright and joyous life. I have no wish to bear witness. She has no pain, no memory of present days that drone on in dreary sameness. Her memories are of fast cars, her own faultless double de clutch which she executed smoothly on tight corners. She believes her car is still in the garage.

Pat, the great driver
Dog in the back seat panting
Heading for the beach.

Pat thinks she can run, walk, dance. Instead the Chinese Nurse hooks pulleys around her wasted body to haul her into a toilet chair. Six thirty shower, eight thirty breakfast, we are lovely and fresh now darling. Pills down there's a girl, don't spit, Doctor will be upset. Teeth glued in, hearing aids in place, Television on, ready for the day. A day of sitting in the chair.

All I do is sit.
My daughter is here to visit
I know she can't stay.

After the visit we see a movie for entertainment. 'The Eye of the Storm' from a story by Patrick White. How fitting—it is about a death of a Mother, his Mother. The family and the nurses are waiting like crows for the spoils left for the living. After seeing this I realise my life, her end, could be much worse. Whose pain is it mine or hers? I never could tell and still cannot.

The Letting Go
Bea Jones

Between your fight against the probable
and acceptance of the inevitable
lies a cobweb line you hold, unseen,
in the pale squeeze of your hand.
This fragile thread has deceptive strength,
not yet weakened by the morphine
that dulls your pain.
With the accusations and denial
that scream out for understanding
I see, still, a fierce glimpse of rebellion
in the confusion of your tired eyes
where fear of the unknown
is too easily expressed by anger.

The next time I see you
I lay my hand gentle
on your brow.
There is no headscarf now.
You gaze with the purity
of an infant's innocence,
yet the wisdom of one all-knowing.
You will travel into a space I cannot enter,
far away from the stale confines
of this weary ward,
blessedly released from the tubes of mortality.
I would wish
that the last second of infinite fragility
that will separate you from those who love you,
will be of all-encompassing peace.

Between your fight against the probable
and acceptance of the inevitable
lay a cobweb line you held, unseen.
Now you have let go, dear friend,
may you glide gently
beyond life's final bend.

You Came Home With Purple Hair
Andrew Sutherland

and your platinum length had disappeared
I saw the darkening mauve you'd made
      your colour in my sternum, cracking
because I know for some queers, a haircut is the best we have
to heal that thing grown tired inside of us.

you came home, cropped purple hair
and clearly this meant *moving on*
      as much as it meant *cutting off*
before you arrived, I spent a choking hour packing what was yours
folded up your shirts, held tight that

stupid husky hat I always made you wear
the photo of your vanished mother
      kept hidden with your socks
wondering if perhaps she hacked her hair away after she'd left you
and how, before too long, I'll be your spectre, too.

you came home to tell me I was not your home
the thought of me had broken in you
      and somehow, you had come to hate
and I can't help thinking it's clichés that cut the deepest
when all I could say was how I loved your hair—

      and you said, *thank you.*

I used to wake each morning and look for you
by signifiers on the bedside table
      your cologne, your portable charger
that bottle of bleach you kept there, ever ready to be used
but I was more afraid of losing than of loss.

now, of course, the bedside table's bare
I train my eyes to hold
      sight of your fading shade
I'm learning how to live Han purple, trailing to Egyptian blue
      and still I keep it growing.

There Let the Waves Lave
Ela Fornalska

. . . but when the new moon's bowl
is storing rain, the pull of time
and sea will cry to me
again.

- From 'Sea Call' by Hone Tuwhare

You will be returned to the river
sink into golden silt
your favourite mud
My hands smell like dog
and I miss you

I meet the waves
and cry straight
into the Bass.

Oh Stanley, hold my broken
heart.
I want to waste away
this afternoon
on your sands
and in this sunshine

Let this grief wash me

I remember her prancing
dance on a withdrawn tide

Today her ashes were delivered
to my mother's door
and I'm all at sea,
alone with this salt

Deep love tows deep loss
This ache is how much
it costs to embrace
a breathing being

Your face is in all the dogs
I see and a smile swells
and I am bathed.

Moving Images
Angela Gardner

I am trying to tell you how it feels.
How at first the camera is at eye-level, seeing the world
human to human. Seeing you, me, eye to eye.
There are forgotten details: the face is familiar
the clothes worn and loved in that nonchalant
crumpled way you had.
Here, the grass beneath our feet is just a bit too long
ragged in its own nonchalance, gone to seed
and it is dusk when everything calls 'Go back!'

Then the camera drone, or I, or you, lifted
and the world below was empty
save for that one figure tossing a white ball.

Away went the white ball and a black ball following.
Away from the white circle flew the black circle
Away and together. Away and together.
The white shape gleaming while the edge of the field
is still blurry, ill defined, low-res, in the last light before
they turn on those huge lights. It didn't make any sense.
And still the tiny figure throwing the white ball
and the black following: its answer, its echo,
its shadow.

The viewpoint was so high, it was dusk
and it was impossible to see the grass as grass.
Nothing to smell or touch, no insect drone or birdsong
no voice-over, no soaring strings.
Just a muffled sound as after the low crump of an explosion.
Or a slippage between sound and moving image
the other end of a telescope, maybe,
all the small sounds a white dot disappearing into dusk.
Everything representation, the words
if they are there, mouthed and soundless.

The field where object and shadow meet
the figure alone on the field.
I am trying to tell you how it feels

                          I take a breath.

Public Grief and Silent Grief
Jadie Kew

Other people's grief is shared and public, it is a sad, communal recognition of loss and a solemn rite of passage. It is acknowledged in shared embraces, celebrated with flowers, music and memories retold, it is unknown by me because I am an orphan.

My grief is silent, solitary and shameful. As the disowned Chinese daughter my very existence is denied. So much in denial are my brothers they did not deem it necessary to inform me of the death of either of our parents. Surely the barest obligation of a sibling is to notify the others of a parental death? It seems a cruel omission of basic humanity. Clutching my birth certificate pointing to her name, the Registrar denied me my mother's Death Certificate because I was not listed as her next of kin. Proving she was my mother was immaterial. Guiltlessly the brothers included my name on the public death notice describing her as my loving mother and the doting nanna of my children. Updating her on my family's existence by letter for more than twenty years without ever receiving a conciliatory reply, my mother had shown no interest in me or my family.

Finally seeking to know if my mother forgot my very existence, having omitted me and the grandchildren she never knew in her detailed list of surviving relatives, my quest for answers ended this year two years after her death, when my brothers' solicitor directed me in writing to never contact them again.

So, I will never know if my demented mother forgot me or did she give deliberate instructions to intentionally omit my existence in her one final act of maternal abuse? Was she denied any opportunity to reply to me when all was controlled by her beneficiary sons? Twenty years is a long time to await a reply, eternity is even longer to ponder these questions.

Making my own way in the world, alone, I chose only to walk away from the conflict, choosing my own sanity over family abuse and disadvantage. I did not harass or mistreat them. I have not robbed or murdered another. Living my life in peaceful isolation with my own family, I chose no more abuse and got on with life.

My grief is not for the parents who wrote their only daughter out of existence. My grief is for that girl's innocence and naivety. My grief laments the parents who never existed for the daughter they have never known. If only there had been one person in my family to hold my hand when times were tough but it was not to be and I will never understand why.

Ghosts leave long dark shadows on your heart.

The Red Scarf
Janey Runci

I'm in a moving tram when I see him, in his wheelchair as always. He's waiting at a traffic light on this wintry day, on the corner of William and Bourke Streets: dark, cold tunnels of streets between the high buildings.

But the intersection is a square of light and sun with a kind of ballet going on, a symphony conducted by the graceful arms of the traffic policewoman dressed in an orange vest in the centre, and waves of pedestrians and cars and trams taking it in turns to flow through the light of the square. It's the William Street turn now, and it's carrying my tram through the intersection. I'm twisted in my seat to keep him in sight.

While he waits he tips his head back to catch the warmth of the sun on his face. You can see he's a tall man, even in the chair. He's wearing a red scarf, not the bulky one I knitted him, that would be at least seven years old by now, but a more stylish one, finer. Merino, I imagine. Elegant. A splash of colour against the dark blue of his jacket. That old pride he took in his clothes has returned. The woman beside him bends slightly as he speaks to her. She smiles and nods, says something in return. He smiles at her. I think she might put her hand on his shoulder, might even bend and kiss his face, feel the coolness of the skin of his cheeks, smell the after shave he loves, but she straightens suddenly, her eyes on the traffic light ahead. She sets off across the road without a backward glance. I put my hand up to my mouth. Surely she'll turn back, at least wave, but it's okay. He's still smiling as he manoeuvres his chair off the footpath onto the street.

Half way across the square his chair skews sideways in the tram tracks. He's bent forward, his hands on the wheels, unable to move. I stand up. The tram is moving further away. He looks smaller and smaller.

'Are you alright?' a kindly-looking woman says as I push my way to the door.

'I need to be there.' I point back to the intersection, but when I look again he's gone. I go to the other side of the tram and see a flash of a red scarf move from the light of the square into the darkness of Bourke Street, and disappear into the moving crowd.

'I thought I saw my son,' I say to the kind woman.

I sit down again and think of him tipping his face to the sun, smiling. It's six years since he died and these moments come to me sometimes, of seeing him, as he might have been. Once they frightened me, now I cherish them.

Today is his birthday. He'd be forty-six. Happy Birthday, darling boy. Happy Birthday.

The Ship
Elisa Hall

It was secret and invisible once the curtain was drawn. Like that time in the change rooms when they'd shared a kiss and slid their hands along each other's skin. Filmed by a security camera which they'd noticed too late. This time there was no camera. This time it was different.

There was a routine. The nurse would come first for the bathing, and then bring the medicine. Afterwards the family would come on the bus between rush hours, hospital parking being too expensive. Trying to be cheery and failing, praying to their god, praying for a miracle. Weeping. Railing.

She would tiptoe in after three thirty. There was an hour before the evening visitors. She would close all the curtains and get on the bed. Steadying herself on her broad Atlas back to hold the long thin frail girl in her arms, mindful of the tubes. There had been a photo of them in earlier days in the same position, this replication a comfort to them both. It was a small bed but they both fit. No-one ever told her to get off. The doctors would come and look, and smile quietly and go away again.

The bed in the curtains was their ship on the ocean. A roiling sea. The feeling was too vast and complicated for language.

The family didn't know she came back, or climbed into the bed and held their beloved. Smelled her downy hair and butterfly kissed her cheeks and stroked her face with eyes full of tears and a fierceness of love displayed only as tenderness. They didn't see the floating into morphine sleep in the timelessness of the end of the day, the light shifting and waning.

'I'm being sent home to die' she said, bravely.

'Yes.' Also bravely.

It was supposed to be weeks but it was only one. Who could measure the abyss of the emptiness. Where once there had been warmth of skin and breath there was silence. No eyelashes, no limbs, no voice.

The funeral people beckoned her to the hearse. To come and touch the glossy coffin when the family weren't watching. Her last touch. She was grateful for their kindness, such a huge kindness. She avoided the grave site; that was for the mother. She held tightly onto her own moments in the hospital, in the bed, and in the change room. She wanted to die too. There was nothing left to be strong for.

She drifted, and dreamed of visitations. Tried to will them. Immersed herself in memory. Touched photographs, kissed photographs. Endured her loss as a tsunami she wasn't sure she could survive. She strode out into the dawning of each day so hard she winded herself, but each day she was still alive and time was passing.

    She dug a hole. Collected the shoes of her beloved, cloaked them in a cloth and buried them. Then planted a tree on top and scattered over the few wisps of hair she'd saved.

The Boy on the Wall
Carolyn Abbs

'A Shepherd Boy', Franz von Lenbach, 1860, oil on canvas

For Alistair, my brother, who lived only four days.

You could tell the little fella didn't make it:
dark hallway, hush on the stairs,
shut door to the room; and within the room
the lowered calico blind, wooden floor
where no-one stepped any more,
or went to the crib—
the sheet as clean and smooth as newly
fallen snow.

In another room (years later)
a girl plays on a warm blue rug.
There's a boy on the wall;
he lies on top of a grassy bank—
arm raised, shading his eyes from the sun—
short trousers, shirt and waistcoat are crumpled
as if he's been there a very long time. The girl
watches him day after day, calling out
Lazybones, Lazybones,
willing him to roll down the slope
to play on the rug.
But he never does.

The glass between them blocks sound,
possibility of touch, any link to the past denied
like the door to the cold room
forever and ever—
silence after Amen.

The River
Rachel Ranton

We used to hunt grasshoppers down by the river.

In the haze of pollen floating and swirling in the sun, 'hoppers bounced around us in the buttery, late-afternoon light. Decades later I can still smell the dust that made the scene blond and grainy like a sepia picture.

When I was small it was impossible to catch 'hoppers mid-jump without squeezing the life out of them, but by my teenage years I was an expert. I could add new inmates to the plastic ice-cream container prison without any escapees.

We used to stride down to the flat, grey rocks on the bank and flick our rods. No chat. Just shared silence stretching out into the valley. When they were biting, I would wind in the silvery trout to flip and flop on the smooth stones. Dad would pin them with his broad, freckled hand before removing the hook to send them back into the icy alpine river.

Last week we had to drive to the river rather than ride our bikes.

Dad had shuffled out of the car whilst I set up a chair for him. I'd twisted the thin piece of silver metal through a 'hoppers exposed abdomen before passing the rod off to dad. We shared the silence; me squatting awkwardly with my cumbersome belly and the baby kicking me, dad grimacing with the effort of sitting in the camp chair, his rod dangling on an angle with a slack line.

Now, there'll be no more fishing.

I walk to our tiny country hospital. The orderly at the station gives me a nod as I head down the corridor. The palliative care ward is a single room. One bed.

As I push open the door dad teases me about my expanding waistline, insisting I can't blame it all on the baby. He's still sharp enough to spot the white flakes from a coconut slice littered across my t-shirt. I offer to smuggle some in for him but he gestures to the tubes hanging out of him.

'Not too much eating going on for me these days,' he says.

Rosemary, dad's nurse, glides into the room and gathers me in a hug.

'It's good to see you, honey' she whispers.

Rosemary checks the machines then leaves us. No longer rationed or on demand, the morphine pumps with a muted click and whispered hiss every few minutes.

Through the window I can see the tall, skinny stalks of grass swaying by the river. In the room, I watch dust bunnies dance in the ribbons of light from the setting sun.

I wait.

It's familiar, but sad; waiting with my dad.

When dad's chest finally stops rising and falling, I don't want to leave him.

Rosemary brings in a monitor and through our tears, she straps the device across my middle and turns up the volume.

The sound of my daughter's beating heart fills the room. I can't wait to take my girl to the river.

The Thieves at the Dam
Tric O'Heare

It is not ash we go back to.
It is grit—like the shelly sand
of childhood's quiet bay beaches
that adheres to the skin
at the end of a good day
and sticks so fast each speck
must be scratched off singly.

There is a finer layer though;
when you winnow a handful
of burnt ground bones
you're left with chalked hands
that you will not want to wash.
This is just a silly life-fact,
a grief-etiquette dilemma
I wrestle with alone today,
unable to reach back in time
with palms whitened by loss
to show you how incomplete
your annihilation has been
so that you could smile and say
Oh well then, I . . .

Down here at the dam's edge
where the mudlarks fossick
I watch a passer-by lean over
the communal garden fence
to steal low hanging fruit.
I am too dumb today for words
and I can't clap to shoo him away
and lose this white dusting
to the too receptive air.
So we move off into our days—
the thief, with his apple-jacket
and me, with my marked hands.

Grief is love
Samantha Geatches

Grief doesn't begin when someone you love dies. I started grieving the day you were diagnosed. I believed with everything I had that if anyone could beat it, it would be you. However, I still grieved for you, and everything you were about to go through. I grieved for the fact that you would never be able to have children. I grieved for the pain this treatment would bring you.

When we were told six months later that the cancer had spread to your lungs, I knew we were in for more of a fight than either of us had ever imagined. The doctor told you that if you had a dream trip you wanted to take, now was the time. But like always, you were determined to beat it and insisted on treatment beginning right away. The holiday could wait until you were better, you said. You never got to take that trip.

I grieved for you then, I knew you would never be fully cured. I grieved for you and the loss of your hair the first morning of the new year when I walked into the bathroom and saw it all over the ground. I grieved for what we used to do on New Years Eve, celebrating with Tequila shots and swimming at midnight, this time you were unable to leave the motel room as you had just undergone your first round of aggressive chemotherapy.

When the cancer went to your brain, I grieved for everything I knew we would never get to do. Travelling the world, raising our families together, taking joint family holidays and going on so many more of our wonderful adventures.

When we got the news you only had days left, my heart broke and the grief came like a tidal wave. I watched cancer take away your ability to hear, and to see and finally to walk.

All that grief was bearable, because you were still here. And then you were gone. And all I wanted was my best friend, the girl who always had that big, beautiful smile on her face, who was always up for a beer or five, went along with anything I suggested no matter how crazy, loved planning holidays, would jump in the pool at midnight on New Year's Eve wearing just your underwear, loved babies, would text me every time you pulled up in my street to ensure the dogs in the street weren't going to bite you, would make a special trip to the local markets just to see if they had banana cupcakes, and who texted me, every day, without fail just to see how my day was.

And that grief had no where to go. And that's when I realised, grief is just love. It's love that has nowhere to go because that person is gone from your life. And so, it manifests in so many other forms: tears, anger, frustration, denial, and I suppose, finally acceptance.

www.ingramcontent.com/pod-product-compliance
Lightning Source LLC
Chambersburg PA
CBHW030257010526
44107CB00053B/1749